G000136908

BIZARRE

TRUE CRIME

VOLUME 6

Ben Oakley

Twelvetrees Camden

Copyright © 2022 Ben Oakley

Bizarre True Crime Volume 6

ISBN: 9798781171491

Independently published.

All rights reserved.

No part of this book may be reproduced, or stored in a retrieval system, or transmitted in any form or by any means, electronic, mechanical, photocopying, recording, or otherwise, without express written permission of the publisher.

Each case has been fully researched and fact-checked to bring you the best stories possible and all information is correct at the time of publication. This book is meant for entertainment and informational purposes only.

The author or publisher cannot be held responsible for any errors or misinterpretation of the facts detailed within. The book is not intended to hurt or defame individuals or companies involved.

Cover design by Ulrich B. & Ben Oakley.

Discover more:

www.benoakley.co.uk

"Despite my ghoulish reputation, I really have the heart of a small boy. I keep it in a jar on my desk." – Robert Bloch, American author of Psycho.

Also by Ben Oakley

Non-fiction

True Crime
Bizarre True Crime Series
The Monstrous Book of Serial Killers
Giant True Crime Books
True Crime 365 series
Year of the Serial Killer

Mysteries
The Immortal Hour: The True Story of Netta Fornario

Mental Health
Suicide Prevention Handbook

Fiction

Harrison Lake Mysteries
Beyond the Blood Streams
Perfect Twelve

Subnet Series
Unknown Origin
Alien Network
Final Contact

Other Fiction
The Mystery of Grimlow Forest

Bizarre True Crime Volume 6

20 loony and ghoulish

true crime stories.

The Bizarre True Crime books can be read in any order. You don't need to have read the previous books to enjoy this one.

1. Murder In Room 1046

In the New Year of 1935, a man checked into a hotel in Missouri, only to have his stay marred by unusual behaviour, bizarre communication, and ultimately, his mysterious death.

2. La Quintrala: The Chilean Elizabeth Bathory

One of history's worst female murderers had a hobby of torturing and killing slaves, but escaped justice due to her wealth and connections, before becoming revered in Chilean culture.

3. Eerie Lady of the Dunes

Read the tale of one of America's most infamous unsolved murder cases, that involves the film 'Jaws', the son of Stephen King, multiple theories, and a mystery that remains to this day.

4. The Skinner

In Poland, a towboat crew found a complete human skin, leading to a 19-year search for a killer who had flayed and skinned his victim alive.

5. The Unsolved Murders of Cabin 28

In a tiny settlement in California, and under cover of darkness, a quadruple murder took place that has echoed throughout the annals of true crime history ever since.

6. Killer in the Cult

A convicted murderer escaped prison and joined a cult to start a new life with a new identity, he remained a fugitive for 15 years until he tried to leave the very cult that had protected him.

7. Abattoir of Katherine Knight

In a rare case of female cannibalism, an abattoir worker stabbed her boyfriend to death, skinned him, put his skin on a meat hook, then cooked his head and other parts to feed to his children.

8. The World's Most Consistent Art Thief

Over a period of six years, a French art thief stole 250 artworks, averaging out to one every 15 days, but he didn't sell for profit, he stole for the love of the art.

9. The Muswell Hill Murderer

The sickening tale of British serial killer Dennis Nilsen, who killed 15 young men, and dissected some of their remains – before flushing them down the toilet and blocking the sewers with flesh.

10. The Great Reality TV Swindle

How a down-on-his-luck homeless man conned fame-seeking wannabes to take part in a year-long reality TV show that didn't exist.

11. The Unusual Death of Chuck Morgan

An escrow businessman went missing twice before being found dead, having apparently shot himself in the back of the head, leading to a mystery of organised crime, a secret life, and cover-ups.

12. First Human Killed By A Robot

In 1979, one of science fiction's most feared scenarios became reality when Robert Williams became the first person in history to be killed by a robot.

13. Satanic Murder of Arlis Perry

A young newlywed went to church to pray and fell victim to an evil killer who did unspeakable things to her body. The killer got away with it for almost half a century until he was finally revealed.

14. Reincarnation of Two Murdered Girls

A year after two sisters were killed in a hit-and-run, their parents gave birth to twin girls, and claimed they were the reincarnated souls of the sisters, in one of the most convincing cases of reincarnation.

15. Killer In the Walls

A creepy intruder terrorised a family by living in the walls of their home and making them think the house was haunted, in a true urban legend that ended with multiple murder.

16. Bodies in the Barrels

In Snowtown, a master manipulator convinced others to help him commit serial murder and dispose of their victims' bodies in barrels of acid, leaving 12 dead, and a town forever tainted by infamy.

17. The Bennington Triangle Disappearances

At least 40 people have mysteriously disappeared in and around an abandoned town, where eerie and unexplained events happen, along with the curse of a nearby mountain said to swallow its victims.

18. The Wendigo Cannibal

A Cree Indian named Swift Runner became possessed by the spirit of the mythical Wendigo then killed and cannibalised his entire family, in the most famous case of Wendigo Psychosis.

19. The Liquid Matthew Clues

Shortly after a murder victim was found in the streets of Miami, detectives discovered a cryptic note inside a plastic bag, seemingly left by the killer, but the clues led them somewhere they didn't expect.

20. The Strange Case of Two Men Who Died Over Dinner

When two Frenchmen enjoying a Summer dinner were found dead at their garden table, police assumed murder was afoot in the small town of Authon-du-Perche, but the truth was far stranger.

Murder In Room 1046

In the New Year of 1935, a man checked into a hotel in Missouri, only to have his stay marred by unusual behaviour, bizarre communication, and ultimately, his mysterious death.

A curious guest

When bellboy Randolph Propst left home for his shift at the Hotel President in Kansas City, Missouri, he wasn't expecting anything less than a normal day at work. Carrying luggage, welcoming guests, and taking bags to guests rooms was all part of the job.

On 2nd January 1935, a single man checked himself into the hotel under the name of Roland T. Owen. Randolph showed Roland to room 1046 on the tenth floor, but didn't carry any bags, as Roland didn't have any. All he had was a comb, a brush, and toothpaste. He also had a strange bald patch on the side of his head.

In conversation, 19-year-old Roland said he had spent the night at the nearby Muehlebach Hotel, now the Kansas City Marriott, but claimed the rate was a little too high for his liking and preferred the inner rooms of the Hotel President.

After placing his comb, brush, and toothpaste on the side, Roland followed Randolph back out the room. Randolph locked the door for him and gave him the key, then watched with curiosity as Roland walked out the hotel and into the city.

Do not disturb

Two days later, on 4th January, switchboard operator Della Ferguson arrived for her shift to find the indicator light was on for room 1046. As the room's phone was off the hook, she called through to the main desk who sent Randolph to check what was needed.

When he arrived at the room, the '*do not disturb*' sign was hanging on the door's handle. He knocked numerous times and a voice from inside told him to enter and then to come in. But the door was locked from the inside, so Randolph went back down to the main desk.

He told Della that the man was probably drunk and to wait another hour before sending him back up. An hour later, another bellboy, Harold Pike, went to the room with a key, and let himself in. The curtains were closed and the room was dark but he could see that Roland was naked on the bed. He put the phone back on the hook and apologised for the disturbance.

Another hour passed, and the operator saw the phone was off the hook again. This time, Randolph went back upstairs to the room and knocked before letting himself in with a key. Inside, Roland was on his hands and knees crawling towards the door. Randolph turned the light on and recoiled in shock.

Roland was covered in blood, as were the walls and ceiling of the main room and the bathroom. Randolph ran back downstairs to raise the alarm. The assistant manager and another hotel worker managed to sit Roland on the side of the bathtub, where they saw his injuries and immediately called the police.

Final words

He had been stabbed multiple times in the chest, with two wounds having punctured his lung, and one barely missing his heart. His wrists and ankles had been tied with electrical cord, with another stretch of cord around his neck.

The bruising around his neck suggested someone had tried to strangle him. He had also been hit over the head multiple times that had resulted in a skull fracture. When police arrived with a doctor, they cut him free from the cords and rested him on the bed.

When asked by the doctor who had done this to him, he answered with a confident '*nobody*'. As he began to pass out from his wounds, he said he had fallen and hit his head on the bathtub. The doctor asked him if he had been trying to kill himself, and Roland responded with '*no*'.

Moments later, he lost consciousness, just as the paramedics arrived. He was taken to a nearby hospital but arrived in a comatose state. Shortly before midnight on 5th January, Roland died of his injuries. And so began a mystery that has perpetuated for close to a century.

Voices

When police investigated the incident, many employees of the hotel came forward to talk about the strange experiences they'd had with Roland and the room itself. The day Roland checked in, one of the hotel maids, Mary Soptic, was doing her rounds on the tenth floor, when she entered room 1046.

Even though she had knocked, Roland was inside the room and the curtains were drawn. She apologised but noted he had an appearance of someone who was scared for his life. He told her to keep the door unlocked as he was expecting someone.

The following morning, on the 3rd, Mary entered the room again to clean it, and Roland was inside the room talking to someone on the phone. She later recalled that she overheard him saying; *'no, Don, I don't want to eat, I'm not hungry. I've just had breakfast. No, I am not hungry.'*

That same afternoon, Mary was giving the rooms fresh towels to replace those taken in the morning clean-up. As she approached room 1046, she heard two male voices. When she knocked saying she had fresh towels, an unidentified man said, *'we don't need any'*.

That same afternoon, Jean Owen checked into the hotel and was given room 1048, next door to Roland's room. It would become a source of much confusion down the line, as Jean had the same surname as the one Roland had given.

That evening, her boyfriend visited her and stayed for two hours, before leaving at around 11pm. She later claimed she heard male and female voices shouting and cursing at each other but couldn't pinpoint exactly what room they were coming from.

Due to her having the same surname and the room next door to Roland, police arrested her for those reasons only. It wasn't until her boyfriend arrived at the police station to back up her story, that Jean was released.

The prostitute

The same night that Jean heard the voices, elevator operator Charles Blocher started his shift. He usually worked the midnight to 8am shift and was used to drunk people coming back from a night out or attending a room party.

He recalled to police that a loud party was taking place in room 1055 but it was not within his job description to quiet them down. He felt guilty taking people to the tenth floor where it had become unusually loud.

At around 1am, a familiar woman entered the lift and asked for room 1026. Charles recognised her as she would often come to the hotel to visit men in their rooms at all hours of the night. He agreed with other staff members that she was a prostitute on out-calls.

Five minutes later, she walked past the lift, which was waiting on the tenth floor, and claimed that her client was not in room 1046, despite having said 1026. She said she was familiar with her client and he was always ready with the light on, before walking off to find the right room.

Half hour later, she took the elevator back down to the lobby. At 4am, the same woman got into the elevator with a new man, and Charles took them to the ninth floor. 15 minutes later, the man went back down to go for an early morning walk. According to Charles, they were the only two people that seemed suspicious at any point during the night.

An alias

An autopsy determined Roland had died of the wounds that had been inflicted, and that they were more than likely caused by another person, rather than self-inflicted. The medical examiner concluded the wounds had been caused between 4am and 5am on the 5th.

The investigation didn't find much evidence in the room besides the voluminous amount of blood splatter on the walls, floor and ceiling. There were no belongings and no extra clothes, with the only items being the comb, brush, and toothpaste that Randolph had seen.

Suicide was touted as a cause of death despite the coroner saying otherwise, but there were no knives in the room. The only other items they found were the two room glasses, one had been chipped and left in the sink, a hairpin, one unsmoked cigarette and a full bottle of diluted sulfuric acid.

Detectives lifted fingerprints, small enough to belong a female, from the room's telephone. All the staff members in the hotel provided fingerprints and personal information but none of them matched the prints on the phone.

When they ran Roland's records, the mystery deepened, as Roland T. Owen was an alias but they couldn't discover who he really was. As the story hit the press, sightings started to come in from all over the city but still, no-one knew his real name.

Sightings

On the night of the 4th, a city worker named Robert Lane, claimed a man had jumped into his vehicle believing him to be a taxi driver, which he wasn't. The man was wearing an undershirt, trousers and shoes, and had a large cut on his arm, that he was holding to stop the blood coming out.

Lane dropped him off at a taxi rank but it wasn't until he read the press stories that his curiosity was roused. Three months later when the funeral was finally held, Lane went to view the body and saw a cut on the dead man's arms that looked remarkably similar to the man who climbed into his vehicle.

He told police he believed the man he picked up was the man who was later killed that night. The problem was that none of the workers in the hotel saw Roland leave his room at any time on the 4th.

Another sighting was by a bar worker in the city, who had seen the dead man drinking with two women on the 3rd and according to what he overheard, they were moving from bar to bar. Other bars in the city seemed to back up the sightings.

As the story went nationwide, a huge number of tips came into the offices of the Kansas City Police Department, and for a while they were inundated with leads that went nowhere. Just a few days after the mystery man died, two more homicides occurred across the city, and the investigation into Roland began to die down.

Ogletree

On 3rd March of the same year, the mystery Roland was due to be buried and a funeral held. Once the funeral home released the schedule, they too were inundated with phone calls and tips. One person said the man would finally be buried next to his sister.

Another claimed the man had been married at the time he had an affair, hence the reason he was killed. The caller had arranged two women and himself to visit him at the hotel to dish out the *'justice that cheaters deserve.'*

The funeral was postponed for three weeks to allow police to once again comb through all of the leads, including flowers that had been sent with different names on. Detectives also posed as gravediggers in the days that followed, in case of unexpected visitors to the burial site.

18 months later, in Alabama, a friend of Ruby Ogletree gave her the latest issue of The American Weekly which contained a rerun of the mysterious murder story. Ruby's friend had noticed something about Roland that may have interested Ruby.

Ruby saw straight away that the unidentified Roland was in fact her son, Artemus Ogletree. She got in touch with the Kansas City PD and they managed to confirm that the unidentified man was in fact her son.

He had left Alabama for California in 1934, hitchhiking his way there. It was the last time she had ever seen him alive. An official identification was quickly given out to the press, but shortly after, the plot, yet again, thickened.

Mystery letters and phone call

Artemus was born in Florida in 1915 and had two siblings. The mysterious bald patch on the side of his head was the result of a childhood accident when hot oil left a large scar. The bald patch was the result of not being able to grow hair after the accident.

Ruby was unaware her son was dead because bizarrely she had been receiving letters from him after he had died. Before his death, Artemus had been writing letters home to let his family know where he was, but in early 1935, Ruby began receiving typed letters from locations across the United States.

She had a feeling something may have been wrong as Artemus didn't know how to type, and the words didn't match his voice or style of writing. In May 1935, she received a letter from New York that said he was going to Europe, and a second one claiming he was on the next ship out.

Then in August 1935, she had received a phone call from a man in Tennessee who claimed that Artemus had saved his life in a fight and that he was now in Cairo living with a woman of great wealth. The man gave his name but it has never been publicly released and there was no evidence that Artemus – or Roland – had left the United States.

In 1937, police discovered Artemus had stayed in a third hotel, the St. Regis in Kansas City. According to hotel records he had stayed in the room with another unidentified man. It led the investigation to believe the man he had stayed with was the man he was overheard calling Don. Since 1937, the investigation went cold but was reopened every now and again as new leads came in.

Theories with little evidence

Due to the lack of solid evidence or suspects, many theories have since arisen. Many suspect he was involved in organised crime, while others suggest he was killed by a jilted lover. Over the years, various letters and phone calls have been received by the Kansas City PD but rather than helping solve the murder, they simply added to the pile of leads that went nowhere.

During his stay in Kansas, Artemus used three different names to check into three hotels, none of which have any bearing on the case. At the first hotel, he stayed there with another man. It's not much of a stretch to assume they were having a sexual relationship.

Artemus may have moved hotels to get away from the man, who followed him to the Hotel President, and was the man heard on the other side of the door, and the one referred to as Don. It's also possible that Artemus may have been having an affair with a married woman and that the other man in the room was her partner, seeking to solve the problem.

An unidentified woman's fingerprints were found on the telephone in his room. There were two possibilities, one that it was the person he could have been having an affair with, the other was the prostitute who had visited the hotel that night.

The theory goes, that after their encounter, Roland had no money to pay her, and she went to get her pimp, who was the man she was seen in the elevator with an hour later. The same man who left the hotel 15 minutes after to get some fresh air and never returned.

Murder mystery

The phone call to Ruby Ogletree was too detailed to have been completely untrue. The man claimed Artemus had protected him during a fight, which verified the city worker's account of an injured man looking like Artemus getting into his vehicle thinking it was a taxi.

It might have been possible that Artemus received his injures during the fight but that wouldn't explain the blood splatted all across the hotel room, which was evidence enough that he had been attacked in the hotel room itself.

Other theories suggest one of the two bellboys or even the maid had killed him and possibly colluded to make it look like someone else. Yet, there was no obvious motive, and in fact motive was something sorely missing from the investigation, for without it, cases are always harder to solve.

Some later theories suggested that Artemus attacked himself, which makes little sense, as he was tied up at both the wrists and ankles. He would not have been able to stab himself, fracture his skull, then tie himself up in the way he was found.

The case of the murder in room 1046 is a mystery that has stood the test of time, simply because the deeper we go, the more confused and mysterious it gets. It's one of those cases that never goes away, in the hope that one day, the truth will come out, and Artemus will finally be laid to rest.

La Quintrala: The Chilean Elizabeth Bathory

One of history's worst female murderers had a hobby of torturing and killing slaves, but escaped justice due to her wealth and connections, before becoming revered in Chilean culture.

La Quintrala

In Bizarre True Crime Volume 3, we dissected the case of Countess Dracula, AKA: Elizabeth Bathory. Much has been written about her and if we are to believe she did indeed kill hundreds of people and wasn't a scapegoat for Hungarian royalty, then she remains one of history's worst killers.

Yet, it's all too easy to forget how diverse the historical true crime landscape is, and those from non-English backgrounds, of which Bathory is the most well-known, never really get the attention that perhaps their cases deserve.

Enter Catalina de los Ríos y Lísperguer, who was said to have been nicknamed La Quintrala due to her bright and flaming red hair. Some researchers write that La Quintrala comes from the Quintral plant, as she used the branches of the plant to whip her victims, and that its flowers were red, like her hair.

Catalina was a landowner and member of the aristocracy in 17th Century Chile. But don't let that upper class innocence fool you. Catalina's life was one of murder, cruelty, and lust.

Her hobby was torturing and killing many of the hundreds of slaves she had under her command. She also tried to kill her father, ordered a priest's assassination, and stabbed another priest in order to redeem her soul.

Colonialism

Born in 1604 to Spanish general Don Gonzalo de los Ríos and his wife María Lisperguer y Flores, Catalina was raised at the tail-end of the Conquest of Chile. María worked as a financer to Spanish Conquistador Pedro Gutiérrez de Valdiva, who became the first royal governor of Chile

Don Gonzalo was already part of the aristocracy and had accumulated a lot of land in Chile's capital, Santiago, where he became one of the colonial society's richest members. He owned various sugar cane farms that utilised black slaves to work them.

For Catalina, growing up in such an environment, where she was protected from the harshness of Chile's slums, and witness to the inhumanity of keeping slaves, it was no surprise she carved out the cruel life she would eventually lead. She had one sister and six brothers, none of whom turned out like her.

Despite being raised in a rich and fortunate family, Catalina didn't get a good education and was known to be illiterate until her death. Her mother was out of the picture when she was young, and she was mostly raised by her father and grandparents.

Catalina grew up to be held in high esteem across Santiago due to her heritage and unusual looks. She was tall, had sheer white skin, green eyes, and memorable flaming red hair. Her heritage was said to have been a mix of German, Spanish, and Incan, though her ancestry is confused when looking at ancestral records. Still, she cut a fine figure in 17th Century Chile.

The dark arts

Her path to cruelty was sped up by known practitioners of witchcraft within her family. Her grandmother,

Águeda Flores, and one of her unnamed aunts, taught Catalina elements of witchcraft when she was a child and imbibed it further into her teenage years.

This combination of privilege and alternative teachings led to Catalina attempting to kill her father when she was just 18-years-old. In 1622, she prepared a dish of chicken for her father and laced it with poison.

Don Gonzalo was bedridden for weeks afterwards but went onto survive. One of Catalina's family members reported the poisoning to law officials but due to a lack of evidence – or her family's influence in the new colonial society – no charges were brought against her.

Aged 22, Catalina married a Spanish Colonel named Alonso Campofrío de Carvajal y Riberos, 20 years her senior. Alonso was paid handsomely by Catalina's grandmother, for taking Catalina off her hands, and in the hope the marriage may have calmed down her violent ways. It was not to be.

Frustrated that the marriage felt forced upon her, Catalina went to the home of the priest who married them and stabbed him in the stomach under cover of night. The priest went on to survive but it was only a taster of what Catalina was building up to.

Assuming control

She had a son with Alonso, who died of natural causes when he was eight-years-old. While Alonso moved from the military to the government and began to rise the ranks there, Catalina was taking lovers in secret.

In 1624, she invited a rich feudal lord to her dwellings. As they fornicated in one of her bedrooms, she slipped out some knives from behind the pillow and stabbed him multiple times. Some of the knives were said to have remained embedded in him when the body was found.

Catalina blamed the murder on one of her black slaves, who was eventually executed in public for the crime.

In 1628, Catalina's only sister died, and she assumed control of her sister's vast estates and land. As more and more land fell under her control, tales of her cruelty were beginning to spread.

She stabbed another potential lover for refusing her sexual advances, then bragged about his sexual inadequacies to others. It was also claimed she cut off the ear of a sexual acquaintance named Martín de Ensenada, and murdered a Santiago Knight in front of another man, after a failed date.

After her father died, Catalina became one of the wealthiest landowners in all of Chile and made her home in one of the vast estates at the base of the Santiago mountains. She even owned land beyond the Andes range to the East of the country.

Like Bathory, her vast amount of land and wealth was a gateway to act out the very darkest of desires. Catalina took full control of the slaves that worked the land she now owned, and in doing so, personally managed the activities of all her estates and properties.

Aggression rising

With no apparent motive, she killed a black slave named Ñatucón-Jetón and left his body to rot in the open air for a fortnight before ordering the remains to be buried. It was said that his body was left on the open fields to put the fear of God into other slaves that lived and worked nearby.

In 1633, a visiting priest, who had heard of Catalina's viciousness, approached her to change her ways, but she stabbed him and beat him to within an inch of his life. When word got around of the priest's beating, many slaves and tenants of her properties eloped into the mountains – which displeased Catalina.

She ordered a militia contingent to head into the Andes and bring back the slaves by force. They were all brought back to her estate at the base of the mountains. Though stories of what happened next have been embellished to some degree, it is known that each of the elopers were punished.

Many were tortured with knives and whipped with the branches of the Quintral parasitic plant. It remains unknown how many were killed during the torture. Catalina paid off local lawyers and judges and protected herself within the veil of her aristocratic family, to avoid prosecution for torture and murder, and it worked – for a while.

Secret investigation and trials

In 1634, a secret investigatory team was put together at the behest of the Royal Audience; the two Spanish colonial courts that represented administrative and political authority.

The lead investigator was Justice Francisco de Millán, who managed to talk to many of the slaves and tenants in secret. Almost all of them accused Catalina of torture, murder, and extreme violence. Some also pointed Francisco to the locations where bodies were buried.

Convinced he had enough evidence, Francisco had Catalina arrested and taken to Santiago for a criminal trial that was to throw the aristocracy into disrepute. She was charged with 40 murders, but it was claimed dozens more had died by her hand.

Due to her influence and wealth, the trial moved slowly, and after being paid off, the judges stalled the case and Catalina was released. At the same time, her husband, though aware of her actions, decided to ignore the stories, and proclaimed his love for her right up until his death in 1650.

She brushed his death off like nothing, as if wiping the blood of her slaves from her shoulder. In 1662, a new trial began, as many officials were scrambling to discover the extent of Catalina's crimes, believing the murders to number vastly more than the 40 originally laid at her feet.

Unknown to officials at the time, Catalina had been getting away with torturing slaves and murdering some of them for almost 30 years, since the first trial was abandoned.

Lavish death and immortality

Catalina became ill, and in 1665, aged 61, died from natural causes, taking many of her dark secrets to the grave. But then something strange happened. In her will, she left 20,000 pesos to the Church of San Agustin for 20,000 masses to be held for her own death and the lives of her slaves and tenants.

She instructed that her assets were auctioned for the benefit of the people of Santiago and the Augustinians. Her funeral was a lavish affair, attracting aristocracy and commoners alike. She was buried in the Church of San Augustín, but the exact location of her tomb remains a secret.

When her exploits and cruelty became public knowledge, many of her estates and properties were abandoned, as people believed her evil spirit resided in them. She lives on in Chilean culture today as both a revered and iconic image.

Despite her violence, she ended up becoming one of Chile's most infamous historical female figures, due to her power within a male-dominated Chile. She was alive at a time when women generally held supporting roles for the men around them.

Her farms, plantations, and estates were crucial to the economy of colonial Chile, and it remains the only possible reason why she was never legally brought to justice, despite the evidence of mass torture, brutality, and murder.

Unlike Bathory, La Quintrala left much of her wealth to the church, Order of St. Augustine, and the people of Santiago, but it still doesn't wipe out the ghoulish nature of her crimes against other humans. She remains one of history's most brutal female murderers, horrific and yet – immortal.

Eerie Lady of the Dunes

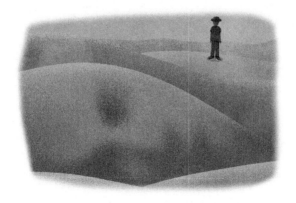

Read the tale of one of America's most infamous unsolved murder cases, that involves the film 'Jaws', the son of Stephen King, multiple theories, and a mystery that remains to this day.

Cold case resurgence

It's important to keep writing and reading about unsolved murder cases, because for the families of the victims, the death of their loved ones hangs like a cloud of pain above their heads, and later their souls, until such time when justice is served.

Many unsolved murders and historical cold cases are today being solved or brought to a logical conclusion by genetic genealogy databases, web sleuths, and a resurgence in cold case investigations. The question that is posed by these cases is ever pertinent – can you, dear reader, solve the mystery?

One such tale of sadness and absence of conclusion is the case of the Lady of the Dunes, the name given to an unidentified female whose body was found in Provincetown, Massachusetts, on 26th July 1974.

The tale of the Lady of the Dunes has evolved to include the theory she was an extra in the film Jaws, as spotted by the son of Stephen King; Joe Hill. To links with infamous mob boss and FBI informant Whitey Bulger, and serial killer Hadden Irving Clark.

Race Point Beach

Tucked away in a cluster of trees on the dunes of Race Point Beach, the decomposed and partially decapitated body of a woman was found by 12-year-old Leslie Metcalfe who followed her dog to the location. She was out walking with her family when the dog ran off and barked.

The girl followed the dog into the dunes and saw what she thought was a dead deer, which wasn't an uncommon sight in the region, but to her horror, she soon realised it was the body of a human. Her family raised the alarm – and an almost fifty year mystery began.

The body was lying face down on a green towel with a blue bandana and blue jeans under her head, as if she was resting on her front.

The woman was nude with pink painted toenails and red hair with a gold-coloured elastic band. Bizarrely, her hands were missing and in place of them someone had put a pile of pine needles.

She was found 15 feet away from a beachside access road, in a location that was commonly used as an entry point to the beach itself, which added to the mystery that she had only just been found, despite the smell of the decomposition and the large amount of insect activity around her.

A medical examiner's report concluded she was between the ages of 20 to 35 and had been dead for approximately two weeks. It has since been changed to include the possibility of death between one week and three weeks.

She was 5 feet 6 inches tall, a slim athletic build, and had extensive dental work carried out on her teeth, most of which had been forcibly removed by her killer. She had been attacked with a military entrenchment tool – a small spade like object – so viciously that her head was partially decapitated.

Investigations

Along with her missing hands and teeth, one entire forearm had been removed. This led the initial investigation to believe they had been taken to hide the identity of the woman. It's possible she had a tattoo on her forearm, or that the killer touched her there, and took it off for his protection.

The killer was most certainly a male, as there were signs the woman had been raped after her death, which then added necrophilia to the mix. Due to the decomposition, any trace of who sexually abused her became lost in the corridors of time.

In close proximity to her body were traces of blood, which meant she had possibly been killed elsewhere and posed at the death scene. Though it looked as if she may have been sunbathing, it would be an awfully strange location – among the trees – to soak up the rays.

When her identity couldn't be solved, and instead of adding another Jane Doe to the ever-growing Seventies list of Jane Doe's, she was nicknamed the Lady of the Dunes. The investigation had little evidence to go on, and the theories were already picking up pace.

The autopsy found a burger and fries in her stomach, which meant she had eaten at a nearby town as there were no close burger places on the beachfront. There was also disagreement between investigators as to whether she was killed at the site or elsewhere.

Those who believed she was killed at the location, pointed to the angle of the head injuries, as if someone had been lying next to her. It assumed that the killer knew the victim well, and if it was her lover, then it stands to reason why they had decided to sunbathe in a more private location.

If the body had been placed at the location then a vehicle would have been used to drive her there. Though there were tyre tracks found 50 metres away from the body, the location was common for vehicles coming into the area, and the police attempted to trace everyone who had visited the area in a car – with no revelation.

Coldest of the cold

Police spent weeks going through hundreds of missing persons cases and interviewed visitors to the area but no-one could find a link to the Lady of the Dunes. There was also no additional evidence found at the scene. As such, the case went very cold.

The first facial reconstruction came five years later and was made of clay. Her body was then exhumed for the first time in 1980 but no new evidence was found. She was buried again but without her skull, which was bizarrely used as a paperweight by the Provincetown chief of police – one hopes as a reminder the case was unsolved rather than anything more macabre.

The second exhumation was 20 years later, in 2000, when investigators hoped that new DNA technology could point to her identity – it didn't. In 2010, her skull was put through a CT scanner for a modern update on a facial reconstruction, but again, the image led nowhere.

With DNA evidence on hand, it was easy to discard many people who had come forward and claimed to be related to her. This included mothers who believed she was their missing daughter, to sister's who believed she was a long-lost sibling.

An uncanny resemblance to a female criminal named Rory Gene Kesinger, who escaped from prison in Massachusetts one year before the body was found, was proved false, after her mother provided DNA. Interestingly, no trace of Kesinger has ever been found, dead or alive.

Links to infamy

Irish mob boss, Whitey Bulger, was linked to the murder, as he was known to remove his victims teeth and had been seeing hanging around with a female matching the woman's description shortly before the discovery.

No evidence has emerged beyond circumstantial to link Bulger to the murder, and he was never known for raping dead women. Yet it could be possible he killed her and someone else had come along and found the body, to be used for their own deviancy.

Two serial killers were linked to the murder. The first was Tony Costa, who killed up to eight women in the late 1960s but was eliminated when it materialised he had died in prison, months before the body was found.

The second, Hadden Irving Clark, who was convicted of two murders, but linked to dozens more, confessed to the murder of the Lady of the Dunes in his prison cell in 2000, and claimed he buried some of the evidence in his grandfather's garden.

Despite the confession, he was ruled out as a suspect at the time. However, years later, he sent a letter to a friend with a drawing of a woman lying on her front and a hand drawn map of an area that looked similar to the woman's location.

When police searched his grandfather's house, they found a bucket buried in his garden, which contained over 200 pieces of jewellery. Clark told them they were trophies from his victims, and if it were to be believed then he may have been the most prolific serial killer in the United States.

Clark suffered from paranoid schizophrenia and experts have ruled out his involvement, claiming his confessions are nothing more than his desire to have control over the police, and to give himself a macabre name as one of the worst serial killers.

Jaws and Joe Hill

Joe Hill, the son of horror author Stephen King, got involved in web-sleuthing after reading a book on the subject in 2015. In the same year, after watching a documentary on the Lady of the Dunes case, he went to watch an anniversary screening of the 1975 film *Jaws*, which had been filmed less than 100 miles away from the location of the body, on the island of Martha's Vineyard.

Fresh in his memory with the facial reconstructions and the clothing found at the scene, including the bandana and jeans, he recoiled in disbelief while watching the film. An extra in one of the beach scenes matched the description of the Lady of the Dunes perfectly.

There were many extras in Jaws, and a lot of them came from the Boston mainland to be on the island when the film was shot in the Spring and Summer of 1974, and as such many people in the crowd scenes were not official extras, and just people who hoped to be in a Hollywood movie.

Hill went to the police with his discovery and they located the scene at 54 minutes into the movie. During a crowd scene on the 4th of July celebrations, there is a woman dressed in a blue bandana and blue jeans with red hair who looks remarkably similar to the dead woman.

Hill said; *'what if the young murder victim no one has ever been able to identify has been seen by hundreds of millions of people in a beloved summer classic and they didn't even know they were looking at her?'* The FBI claimed that 'odder ideas' have solved cold cases. Interestingly, no-one has come forward to claim they know who the extra was.

Almost 50 years after her death and with large frequent investigations taking place, no new evidence or information has come to light, and the Lady of the Dunes has become less of a cold case, and more of a case that remains frozen in time.

Two things happened on the beaches of Massachusetts in 1974; a blockbuster movie was made, and a woman was brutally killed. Both, it seems, have stood the test of time, and may in some part be inextricably linked forever.

The Skinner

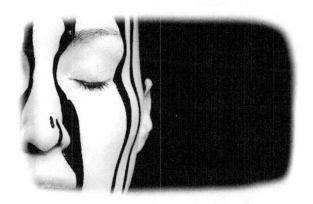

In Poland, a towboat crew found a complete human skin, leading to a 19-year search for a killer who had flayed and skinned his victim alive.

Missing

Katarzyna Zowada was a 23-year-old religious student at the Jagiellonian University, close to Kraków in Poland. She had been suffering from depression since the death of her father two years earlier.

To help her way through education, she chose to study psychology to aid her depression but when that didn't work, she turned to a course of religious studies. Her friends described her as sad and withdrawn but was considered a nice person who was easy to get on with.

Katarzyna was due to meet her mother at a psychiatric unit in Kraków on 12th November 1998, where she was being treated for her depression. When she failed to turn up, her mother filed a missing person's report.

An investigation began but went cold quickly as investigators had nothing to go on, and due to Katarzyna's depression, passively concluded she had run away or taken her own life somewhere. Just two months later on 6th January 1999, investigators were proven wrong – very wrong.

Suit of skin

A towboat crew on their usual route along the River Vistula, the longest river in Poland, discovered something caught in the propeller. The captain was used to items in the river jamming the propeller, with the usual culprit being large tree branches.

When crew members uncoiled the blockage, they were hit with a god-awful smell and threw the strange object onto the floor of the boat. When they looked closer, they noticed a human ear sticking out, and called the police.

The remains were examined and tested, with new DNA technology proving they were the human remains of Katarzyna. But when they looked closer, they discovered something horrific. Police and the initial medical examiner assumed Katarzyna had got caught in the propeller, which had led to the horrific state of the body.

Aside from her left leg found in the river nearby, there was no body at all, only skin. They made the shocking discovery that the skin had been removed from the torso on purpose, and the limbs and head had been removed. Grimly, it was possible to wear the skin as a macabre skin-suit, which may have been the killers intention.

19 years

In May 1999, the medical examiner's office who had identified the skin, received the body of a man with a severed head. The killer, known only as Vladimir, was the son of the victim, and prior to his arrest had been seen wearing a mask made of his father's face.

Investigators noted the similarities between the murder of Vladimir's father and the way in which Katarzyna had been killed. Despite the clear link, there was not one single shred of evidence that Vladimir was involved in Katarzyna's killing. Vladimir was sentenced to 25 years for his father's murder.

In 2000, the investigation into Katarzyna's murder slowed down as no suspect was found but continued to follow leads when they came in. In 2012, the remains were excavated and authorities enlisted the help of specialist Portuguese and American 3D analysts and DNA experts to help with a more thorough examination.

The new investigation concluded Katarzyna had been beaten, flayed with a sharp knife, and skinned while she had been alive, ultimately dying of blood loss when her organs were ripped out of her.

In 2014, the FBI were acquisitioned to help build a profile of the killer. They reported that the killer was a sadist who enjoyed harassing women, and would most likely have a prior criminal record, possibly having served jailtime. He also would have been known to Katarzyna.

In 2016, professor of forensics and expert in signs of human torture, Duarte Nuno Vieira, of the University of Coimbra concluded she had been tortured before her death. He also amazingly deduced that the killer was highly trained in a specific variation of martial art.

Then 19 years after the murder, in 2017, a team of cold investigators, backed up with the profiles and building evidence, were given a breakthrough that would solve the case.

The Skinner

Since the recovery of Katarzyna's skin, the investigation had looked at many possible suspects and one that interested them the most was Robert Janczewski but they had no evidence to go on. He had been raised in a strict religious household and was beaten by his father up until his teen years.

As a child, he was known to abuse cats, dogs, and other small animals. Which apparently wasn't flagged when he got a job at the Kraków Institute of Zoology, where he was able to watch the process of preparing animal skins for study. He was fired the day after he killed all the rabbits in the lab during his shift.

He then had a brief stint at a dissecting lab where he had contact with human corpses, before being fired for indecent behaviour. He also made multiple visits to Katarzyna's grave while dressed in various women's clothes.

In 2017, when Robert was 52, the police received a letter from a close friend of his. Though the letter has never been made public, the details within it led to his arrest, and he was charged with Katarzyna's first-degree murder.

He also fitted the psychological profile from the FBI and the report from Professor Viera, in that he was known to Katarzyna, hated women, and was trained in an obscure Eastern martial art. Due to the horrific nature of the case and the details of the crime, law officials requested a closed trial, which was granted.

It's public knowledge that Robert was incarcerated but no location has been disclosed, which might mean that he has been sent to a maximum security psychiatric hospital, where it's likely he will remain for the rest of his life.

The Unsolved Murders of Cabin 28

In a tiny settlement in California, and under cover of darkness, a quadruple murder took place that has echoed throughout the annals of true crime history ever since.

Keddie Murders

Keddie is a small settlement in Plumas County, California, a short distance from Quincy. Its only calling card is the Keddie Wye; a railroad junction named after Arthur Keddie and completed in 1909. The population of the settlement has consistently remained below 100.

Of course, there is something else the town is known for – cold-blooded unsolved murder. From 1978 until 1981, the area had become a bustling resort location for tourists, thanks to the Keddie Resort, a collection of 33 rustic wooden cabins.

They were rented out for a little under $200 (USD) a month, and attracted hikers for the long wooded trails, along with the nearby stream that was perfect for fishing. On 11th April 1981, the quaint settlement was tainted by bloody murder.

Known as the Keddie Murders, the unsolved quadruple murders took place in house 28, later known as cabin 28. On the morning of 12th April, 14-year-old Sheila Sharp returned from a friend's house and entered cabin 28. What she saw inside changed her life forever.

New beginnings

36-year-old Sue Sharp and her five children had been living in cabin 28 for five months, having moved to the area from Connecticut, to be close to her brother. She rented a trailer from her brother before moving to cabin 28 at the Keddie Resort.

Sue moved to California as she had separated from her knowingly abusive husband, James Sharp, who was against her taking the children. For five months, everything had been going well at the resort, and the children had begun to settle in.

Sheila had made some friends in the town and so it was not uncommon for her to stay at a friend's house for sleepovers. On that fateful Spring morning, Sheila walked back from the sleepover and entered through the front door of the cabin.

She discovered the body of her mother, her 15-year-old brother, John 'Johnny', and his 17-year-old friend, Dana Wingate. All three had been tied up, brutally stabbed, and beaten to death with a claw hammer. Sheila's 12-year-old sister Tina was nowhere to be seen.

Her youngest brothers, five-year-old Greg and ten-year-old Rick were asleep in one of the bedrooms with a friend, Justin Smartt. All three victims had been tied up with electrical cord and wiring around their ankles and wrists. Sue was found covered by a bloody yellow blanket.

Sheila ran away from the cabin screaming at the top of her lungs. She collapsed through the door of her friends cabin, who in turn raised the alarm and called the sheriff's department. Suddenly, tales of murder had broken the peace and serenity of Keddie and would forever be tarnished by it.

A violent end

It wasn't until the police were called that Sheila realised her two youngest brothers and their friend were still in the cabin. She and some of the neighbours went to the side of the property and helped them out through a window. All three had slept through the entire night.

The Plumas County Sheriff's department arrived on the scene and began the arduous task of piecing together exactly what had gone down in cabin 28. Sue and Johnny had been stabbed numerous times and their throats had been slashed.

Sue had also been beaten with the butt of a rifle, and when a coroner checked her body, it appeared she had put up a good fight. She was also found nude with her underwear stuffed into her mouth. Her head had been bashed in with the claw hammer, as had Johnny's.

The knife used to stab them was found just metres away with the blade bent, such was the force with which they had been stabbed.

A bloodied hammer was also found nearby. Dana had been beaten to death with the hammer and manually strangled.

Blood splatter was found on the wallpaper, the ceiling, and all across the furniture in the living room. Sue's bare feet and Johnny's shoes were bloodstained, meaning they had been standing up in pools of blood at some point before being finally killed.

Yet, Tina was still nowhere to be seen. After the autopsies, the missing girl became the focus of the investigation, as detectives began piecing together the events the day before the murders.

Silent screams

Shortly before noon on the 11th of April, Sue, Sheila, and Greg had left the nearby Meeks residence to pick up Rick, who was playing baseball at the Ganser Field in nearby Quincy. As they drove back to Keddie, Sue picked up Johnny and Dana who were hitchhiking.

At around 3pm, Johnny and Dana hitched a ride back along the five mile route into Quincy where they had plans to visit friends for the evening. As there was nothing to do in Keddie, Quincy had a lot more going for it with a population of just under 2,000.

That evening, Sheila made plans to spend the night at a sleepover with her friend at the Seabolt cabin, the cabin next to hers. Tina had gone with Sheila at 8pm to the Seabolt cabin and asked her mother if she could stay the night like Sheila was going to.

Sue refused, and Tina returned to cabin 28 around 9.30pm. At around the same time, Johnny and Dana were witnessed in the downtown area of Quincy near the Gold Pan Motel, before seen hitching a ride on the route back to Keddie at around 10pm.

It was the last time they were ever seen alive, and there has never been any witnesses to claim how they had got back to the resort or who picked them up. Police were baffled as to why no-one at the resort had heard the murders taking place.

Aside from a nearby cabin claiming to have heard muffled screaming at around 1am, none of the closer cabins had heard anything from cabin 28, one being only ten feet away. Even more baffling that the youngest boys had supposedly slept through it.

Team of investigators

There was no sign of forced entry but the telephone had been taken off the hook and the cord had been cut. Some shoes, a toolbox containing various tools, and Tina's jacket were missing from the cabin, but investigators ruled out robbery as a motive.

Police concluded the murders had been planned and had involved at least two attackers, with one of them having brought a claw hammer into the cabin with them. Another hammer, and both knives were ones that were already in the cabin.

The investigation put out a state-wide missing persons profile for Tina Sharp, who still hadn't shown up. Police stated that whoever had carried out the murders would have been covered head to toe in blood splatter, due to the violence inflicted on the victims.

In the first fortnight following the murders, eight hardened investigators worked on the case around the clock, and even implemented a secret witness program to convince any witnesses to come forward so they could get even the slightest lead.

As weeks turned to months, and months to years, the investigation resorted to responding to leads as and when they came in. Then Justin came forward and claimed that he had woken up at some point in the night and witnessed the murders.

Justin's hypnosis

Despite originally claiming to have slept through the night, Justin Smartt told investigators that he had witnessed the murders through the bedroom door. He later changed his story and said he dreamt about it.

Convinced they had something anyway, investigators put Justin under hypnosis. He was able to recall the faces of two men, both wearing glasses, one with a moustache and one with long shoulder-length hair.

One of the men had a pocket-knife that he used to stab Sue in the chest. He also remembered that the same man had a hammer with him. Then Johnny and Dana entered the cabin and got into a fight with the two men, who easily overpowered the two teens.

Shortly after, Tina entered the living room, walking in on the murders in progress and was swiftly taken out the back door by one of the men. A composite sketch of the two men were released to the public based on the boy's dreams, but unsurprisingly they went nowhere.

A psychologist and psychiatrist evaluated Justin extensively and concluded that he may well have witnessed the attack and as a psychological defence mechanism, had converted the crime into a dream. The details given under hypnosis were extraordinarily vivid and detailed.

Tina Sharp is found

One of the first and still the main suspect was Sue's neighbour, Martin 'Marty' Smartt, who lived two cabins away with his wife, Marilyn, both parents to Justin. Marty and Marilyn were going through a troubled patch in their marriage, and it later emerged that Sue would interfere in their relationship, which angered Marty.

At some point over the previous Winter, Marty's friend, ex-convict, John 'Bo' Boubede had moved into the Smartt cabin, which had caused a deeper divide between the bickering couple.

At the time, both men were ruled out due to lack of evidence, even though Marty oddly claimed that someone had stolen a claw hammer from his home. Despite massive media interest, the case went cold until three years later when a grim discovery was made.

On 22nd April 1984, a bottle hunter was carrying out his hobby when he came across human remains near Feather Falls, 50 miles from Keddie. Unsure what they had, investigators sent the remains off to be identified.

A medical examiner confirmed through dental records that the remains belonged to 12-year-old Tina Sharp. There had been speculation in the press that the attack was a cover to get hold of Tina, and much public interest had been generated on the belief that Tina may have still been alive.

The discovery of her body was a hammer blow to the investigation and those who hoped for a happy ending for the 12-year-old. Curiously, the examiner concluded she had been killed seven months after her disappearance, in around November 1981.

Due to decomposition, a cause of death could not be determined, but it was concluded that she too had been murdered. Some of her clothing was found nearby, along with an empty medical tape dispenser.

Investigation running on empty

One theory that was run at the time, involved Johnny and Dana returning from Quincy to walk in on Sue being attacked, which resulted in a fight where the two teens were overpowered and also killed, much like Justin's statement under hypnosis.

But the lack of forced entry led some to consider that whoever had picked Johnny and Dana up hitchhiking had followed them to the cabin and pushed their way inside. The pair were known to have attended a party in Quincy where drugs were being used.

This meant that any potential witnesses refused to come forward for fear of getting in trouble themselves for drugs. Investigators also ran the theory that two men from the party had followed them back to the cabin. There were some reports that there were two men acting weird around the two boys but nothing could be confirmed.

A usual theory for the 1980s was that of the involvement of a cult, Satanic or otherwise. The Satanic Panic of the Eighties was in full swing and the fear of such groups were doing the rounds on talk shows and the news. Again, no evidence was found.

In 1996, serial killer Robert Joseph Silveria Jr. confessed to the Keddie murders. He had drifted through the United States during the Eighties, killing drifters on the railroads. He confessed to 28 murders, was suspected of 17, and convicted of two. It turned out he was in custody for a traffic offence, the night of the Keddie murders.

Smartt complex

In 2004, cabin 28 was demolished and no property has ever been rebuilt on the site. Four years later, in 2008, Marilyn Smartt, who had since divorced from Marty, claimed that Marty and Bo were responsible for the murders.

She stated that she had left Marty and Bo at a Quincy bar at around 11pm and returned home to go to sleep. She woke up at 2am to find the two men burning unknown items in the wood stove. It was suspected to be clothing worn by them that night.

In 2013, a new sheriff brought some of the original investigators back from retirement to reorganise the Keddie reports, boxes, evidence, and statements. The regrouping of the investigation led to the discovery of a hammer, found by a metal detector, in a pond near to where the Keddie Resort had been.

It matched the hammer that Marty claimed was inexplicably stolen from his cabin. In 2016, the investigators stumbled upon an overlooked piece of evidence in the boxes. It was a letter written from Marty to Marilyn, weeks after the murders, and as they were separating.

The letter read; '*I've paid the price of your love & now I've bought it with four people's lives.*' Investigators simply overlooked it at the time. Marilyn later confirmed that she had never received the letter but that it was her ex-husband's handwriting.

A fading hope

Marty was said to have hated Johnny Sharp for unknown reasons, and blamed Sue for everything bad in his own marriage. Also in 2016, it was revealed that Marty had left Keddie shortly after media interest had died down, and drove to Reno, Nevada, where he set up a new life.

An article in the same year criticised the original investigation and claimed there were so many schoolboy errors that took place, including not looking into Marty more deeply as a suspect. Around the same time, a counsellor came forward, who Marty had visited.

He claimed that Marty had admitted he killed Sue and Tina but had nothing to do with the two boys. He said that Marty killed Tina as she had recognised him and to prevent her identifying him to police. Marty claimed that Tina had witnessed the entire thing.

Unfortunately for cold case investigators, Marty died of cancer in June 2000 in Oregon, and John 'Bo' Boubede died in Chicago in 1988. It has long been suspected that Marty did indeed kill Sue and Tina, and that Bo killed Johnny and Dana when they walked in on the murder of Sue.

However, both men passed lie detector tests in the original investigation, and there is no evidence beyond a counsellor's revelations and a letter that was mysteriously overlooked. Neither of the two were arrested at the time and some researchers believe their involvement to be nothing more than unfounded rumour.

In 2018, new DNA evidence suggested there may be a living suspect who had ties to the murders but the investigation ended there with no ultimate revelation.

As it is, the murders at cabin 28 remain unsolved, but there is hope that one day, a new piece of evidence will point to the real killer – a hope that is slowly fading.

Killer in the Cult

A convicted murderer escaped prison and joined a cult to start a new life with a new identity, he remained a fugitive for 15 years until he tried to leave the very cult that had protected him.

Convicted

Not many people knew they had a convicted murderer and fugitive living among them. For years, residents in the historic tin-mining town of Herberton, Queensland, Australia, were living with Luke Andrew Hunter, who had been on the run for 15 years.

In 1990, Hunter was convicted in a Queensland court of the pre-meditated murder of his lover's husband, 36-year-old Brian Phillip Nagle, who he shot in the head with a high-powered rifle.

After the murder, the then 21-year-old Hunter buried the body in a shallow bushland grave and removed personal items to make it look like Brian had left on his own accord.

Hunter moved in with Brian's wife and lived in her house for a whole month until Brian's body was uncovered by landscapers in the region. Hunter was arrested and charged with the murder but claimed he had done the right thing, as Brian had raped and beaten his wife on multiple occasions.

He was sentenced to 21 years in prison for the murder, to serve out his time at the Borallon Correctional Centre. There, he accustomed himself to the routines of the guards, gathered the tools needed to escape, and spent time putting a plan into action.

In 1996, he escaped by cutting through a perimeter fence with a bolt cutter stolen from the prison laundry. He was last seen running away from the prison, dressed in prison clothes and carrying the bolt tool.

Jesus Group

Hunter had become Queensland's number one fugitive, and Australia's number four most wanted. It was no surprise he wanted to lay low, as the country's press were having a field day that someone had managed to escape from prison, not least a murderer.

When he escaped, Hunter managed to elude authorities by hiding out with a religious group called the North Queensland Jesus Group of Watsonville, which was south of Herberton. It was there, he hid in plain sight, familiarising himself to the group's ways as the heat on him died down.

He discovered freedom in the free love, open sex, and spiritual order of the reclusive and polygamist Jesus Group, who followed the ancient order of Aramaic religions. He lived in a unit on the communal farm, worked the land, carried out maintenance, and joined in prayer when the ram's horn was blown.

While hiding out with the group, he slightly changed his appearance and apparently found God while with them. He created a new identity and called himself Ashban Cadmiel, which in old Hebrew meant he was a Judahite thief who was stoned to death. Unusual choice, to be sure.

18 months later, the cult helped him secure official documentation for the new persona he had developed and assisted him in getting a job at the local hospital. For the next 13 years, Hunter worked at the hospital in close proximity to patients.

While the whereabouts of the fugitive remained a mystery to police, he was a familiar and friendly face with the patients at his work, where he tended to the garden and cleaned the wards. He also helped move dead bodies from the wards to the morgue.

Operation Blaze

Six years after his escape, his part-time position was promoted to full-time as an operational services officer, and his average wage was around $60,000 (AUD) per year from then until his capture. At the trial for his recapture, it was estimated he had earned around $650,000 (AUD) in earnings from the hospital.

While working at the hospital, Hunter and his girlfriend remained close with the Jesus Group, living in one of their units. His life on the run fell apart when they decided to leave the cult to raise money for African Children.

In February 2011, using an anonymous tip-off, police ran a three-day operation with a ten-man team to find enough evidence to arrest him. They called the investigation; Operation Blaze. Though the tip-off was anonymous, it was suspected to have come from someone inside the cult.

They contacted the local hospital and searched the maintenance shed, and Hunter's locker, for evidence that it was indeed the fugitive they had been after all that time. While he was out jogging in the early hours of the morning, a team of police approached him and arrested him on the spot, with Hunter going easily.

They worked out that he had assumed a number of aliases with enough false documentation to find official work, which is how he landed the hospital gig – aided by the cult. Residents of Herberton were stunned at news of the killer in their midst but their reactions were varied.

Hunter became the hunted

Many claimed he was young when the murder took place and it had been carried out under the banner of passion and forbidden love. His landlady claimed he was a '*really lovely man*', and that she would even give him a character reference.

Though the small town was shocked at the fact a murderer had lived among them, they related tales to the local press about how helpful he was, and how he was always seen out jogging, where he'd greet people on his run.

The Jesus Group were later investigated for allegedly harbouring Hunter but they claimed they had no idea who he was, and that their community was open to all, regardless of their backgrounds and history.

The hospital was also investigated and involved the Health Minister Paul Lucas, who came under fire for the hospital not having run proper checks. However, Hunter – as Ashban – was employed in 1997 when criminal checks were not routinely undertaken.

Even if latent criminal checks were carried out, Hunter had used a false identity, and with the help of the Jesus Group, he had all the documentation to show it. It meant that a check would not have brought back anything untoward.

Hunter was sentenced for a crime he had committed, and by his own actions sought to evade that sentence. It remained justice for Brian Nagle's family, that Hunter was recaptured to see out the rest of his sentence. He was released on parole ten years later, in 2021.

For a while, Hunter had become the hunted, and fallen prey to the snare of justice.

Abattoir of Katherine Knight

In a rare case of female cannibalism, an abattoir worker stabbed her boyfriend to death, skinned him, put his skin on a meat hook, then cooked his head and other parts to feed to his children.

Cannibals

Cannibals are rare, so rare that some psychologists don't believe they exist as a killer type and are instead addendums to a disturbed mind. Cannibalism is defined as the practice of eating the flesh of one's own species and can also include the consumption of blood.

There have been few killers with a cannibalistic nature in the modern era, including Dennis Nilsen, Andrei Chikatilo, Jeffrey Dahmer, Joachim Kroll, Nikolai Dzhumagaliev, and Hadden Clark, among others.

Though all disturbing for the brutality of their crimes, there is perhaps no scarier facet of society than when a woman decides to kill and cannibalise her victim – and hang the victim's skin on a meat hook in the house they shared.

That's exactly what happened when Australian abattoir worker Katherine Knight decided she'd had enough of her boyfriend. When police arrived at the property they were met with a sight they would never forget.

Bad blood rising

Katherine was a textbook example of a killer whose childhood was marred with violence and abuse. Her mother, Barbara, was from Aberdeen, New South Wales, and had married Jack Roughan but all was not well with their marriage and Barbara cheated on Jack with Ken Knight.

When the affair became public knowledge, pressure from the locals forced Barbara and Ken to leave the area for the town of Moree, 230 miles (375km) north of Aberdeen. Barbara's four sons stayed with Roughan.

While in Moree, Barbara and Ken had four more children together, including twin girls in 1955. Katherine was the younger of the two twins. Four years later, Jack died, and two of the sons he shared with Barbara, moved into the Knight household in Moree.

Ken Knight became a violent alcoholic who resorted to beating Barbara on a near-daily basis, along with raping her in front of Katherine. In her formative years, Katherine was sexually abused by family members, and witnessed open sexual encounters with her mother and brothers.

Barbara was known to talk explicitly about her sexual encounters to Katherine, and once told her that she hated men but deserved the beatings and rapes. The only comfort Katherine took was with her uncle, Oscar Knight, who took his own life when Katherine was 14. She later claimed that his ghost would visit her on occasion.

During her school years, Katherine became a loner and a bully, and was able to manipulate those around her. At the age of 16, she took a job that would be forever linked with the crime she committed – cutting up offal at the local abattoir.

Unchecked violence

She was known to take her butcher's knives home to hang above her pillow, claiming she may well have use for them if needed. In 1974, aged 19, Katherine married her co-worker David Kellett. Both of them enjoyed heavy drinking and getting into fights at the local bars.

On their wedding night, Katherine strangled Kellett to within an inch of his life and explained it away by saying it was because he had fallen asleep after only three sex sessions. The violence continued, and one year later, Katherine smashed him over the head with a frying pan.

Fearing for his life, he stumbled to a neighbour's house where emergency services were called. It turned out that Katherine had fractured his skull with the pan but she then manipulated him and convinced him to drop any charges against her.

Just a few months later, in 1976, and shortly after the birth of their first child, Kellett escaped the violent clutches of his wife and moved in with another woman. The next day, Katherine was arrested for violently bouncing a pram around – with the two-month old Melissa inside.

She was admitted to a psychiatric hospital, diagnosed with depression, and treated for many weeks. When she was released, she took her daughter to a nearby railway, rested her small body on the tracks – and walked away.

After stealing an axe from a landowner, she stomped into town and threatened to kill anyone who looked at her the wrong way. At the same time, a local homeless person, who was picking berries near the train line, saw the baby on the tracks and picked her up seconds before a train passed.

Despite the threat to the child and her threats towards others, Katherine only spent one night in a psychiatric hospital and checked herself out the next day. It appeared that early on, her violent outbursts and murderous ways were going unchecked by officials.

Out of control

The violent incidents didn't stop there. In the same year, Katherine slashed the face of a woman she kidnapped to drive her to Queensland to find Kellet. The woman escaped, and when police arrived, Katherine was holding a small boy hostage.

She was yet again taken back to the psychiatric hospital, and yet again released just weeks later. Bizarrely, Kellet returned to her when he found out that she had planned to kill him. He said it was to support her in her mental health, but quickly had another daughter with her.

For many years, things had started to calm down, but in 1984, Katherine left Kellet and moved to Muswellbrook, just a few miles from where her mother had been born in Aberdeen. Due to a back injury, she had left work at the abattoir and was claiming disability benefits. Though she kept all of her butcher's knives.

In 1986 she met her next partner, David Saunders, and became immediately jealous of what he was up to when she wasn't around. A year later, she held his beloved dingo puppy up in front of him and sliced the dog's throat with a knife, as a warning it would happen to him if he cheated on her.

Throughout their relationship, she hit him with a frying pan, stabbed him in the stomach, smashed him in the face with an iron, and cut up all his personal belongings. Saunders later went into hiding, and bizarrely, Katherine was issued an injunction against him after she lied and said he was beating her – to stop him seeing their daughter.

Katherine had one more relationship that didn't go well, before meeting John Price in 1995. She lived in his house with his children for three years until 1998, when the violence and abuse towards him escalated.

Escalation to murder

John was already aware of Katherine's temper and violence, but for the first couple of years, their relationship was going well. Then, in 1998, he refused to marry her, which pitted her against him. She got him fired from his job at the local mine.

A few months later, John restarted the relationship with her, but refused to allow her into his home, where his daughters from another relationship were staying. The fighting got worse and his friends refused to see him if he insisted on remaining with her.

In early February 2000, 44-year-old Katherine stabbed John in the chest and she was arrested but again nothing came of it. On 29th February, John took out a restraining order against Katherine, and told his new co-workers that if he didn't turn up for work the next day then he might have been murdered.

John spent the evening with neighbours and returned home at around 11pm. At around midnight, Katherine entered the property while John was sleeping. She watched TV, had a shower and then woke him up for sex. He fell asleep shortly after.

Moments after he had fallen asleep, Katherine stabbed him in the chest multiple times. Somehow, John managed to escape the bedroom and crawl to the front door, leaving a trail of blood behind him. Katherine dragged him back and continued stabbing him. John ultimately died of 37 stab wounds. Some say he was lucky to have died then, for what happened next was animalistic.

The horror

Katherine took the knives from above her bed and proceeded to remove the skin from John's entire body, in one piece. She hung his skin like a curtain on two meat hooks she installed in her living room.

After decapitating the body, she placed his head in a large pot on her stove and boiled it along with a variety of vegetables. She also cooked some of his flesh to mix in with the dish. When she was done, she made up the dining table and placed the pan with the cooked head in the middle.

She served the dish with gravy, potatoes, and additional parts of his body. She created place mats out of cardboard and wrote a little message to John's son and youngest daughter before setting a place for them.

When John didn't arrive to work the next day and heeding his warning of having been murdered if he didn't turn up, an employee went to the house to check on him. With a neighbour, they looked through the windows and saw blood on the floor.

The first two officers on the scene were Scott Matthews and Graham Furlonger, who arrived to carry out a welfare check on John. They broke the door down and Graham entered the property first. In front of him was a curtain – at least that's what he thought it was.

As he neared the curtain, he then assumed it was a blanket hanging from the ceiling but then came the horrifying truth. As he pushed the blanket aside, he noticed blood on his hand, and then looked up – it was John's skin hanging from the ceiling.

The Nanna

As they traipsed slowly along the hallway, they saw blood splatter everywhere, on the walls, the floor, the doors. As they approached the kitchen, they saw the dish that Katherine had served up. Panicked, the two officers called in for all the back-up that was available.

In the garden, they found the rest of John's body, which had been thrown out for the dogs. There were sections of his buttocks that had been fried and thrown into the yard. The officers crept up the bloodied stairs to the bedroom, where they found Katherine in a coma on the bed.

She had taken an overdose of pills in an apparent suicide attempt but was still very much alive.

Paramedics transferred her to the hospital, where she was able to make a full recovery – to face the justice that was about to come her way.

Despite psychiatrists confirming she was suffering from severe mental health issues and could have used that as a defence, Katherine wanted to plead guilty but no reason was given as to why. She claimed she had amnesia and didn't remember killing him but knew she must have done.

During the media storm that followed, medical examiners noted the expert precision with which she removed the skin, including facial features. This enabled the skin to be reconnected to the body for the funeral service.

In 2001, Katherine was the first woman in Australian history to be sentenced to life in prison without the possibility of parole. She filed an appeal five years later but it was dismissed immediately.

She lives out the rest of her days at the maximum security Silverwater Women's Correctional Centre, where she refers to herself as *The Nanna*, on a mission to sort out the woes and disputes of other convicts. Since being sentenced, no member of her family has been to see her.

Katherine Knight remains one of Australia's worst criminals, male or female, and her final act of violence remains one of the most disturbing in recent true crime history. That she has never shown remorse, goes to show that maybe, there really is true evil in the world.

The World's Most Consistent Art Thief

Over a period of six years, a French art thief stole 250 artworks, averaging out to one every 15 days, but he didn't sell for profit, he stole for the love of the art.

Entranced

On a cold March day in 1995, 24-year-old Stéphane Breitwieser and his girlfriend Anne-Catherine Kleinklauss were visiting the medieval castle of Gruyeres, Switzerland, famous for its cheese. While walking through the castle, they found themselves alone in the Bella Luce room.

On the wall was a small painting, a portrait of an unknown woman from the 18th Century German painter Christian Wilhelm Dietrich. Suddenly entranced by the unknown woman – in front of his girlfriend – he decided he needed to have it.

Anne-Catherine kept watch as Stéphane found the hooks on the back of the painting, lifted it off and slipped it inside his jacket. It was a simple process that he would use for almost every piece of art he stole.

For the next six years, Stéphane ended up stealing almost 250 artworks and other exhibits from 172 museums and galleries around Europe. For the first few years, he was supported by Anne-Catherine, who served as a lookout and diversion.

Slicing them out the frame

Some of the works he stole were worth millions but he never had any intention of selling, in fact, he later claimed he stole the artworks for safe-keeping from other thieves, as the art was too easy to steal.

He worked as a waiter, travelling around Europe, and over a six-year period was stealing a piece of art every 15 days on average. Stéphane referred to himself as an art connoisseur and built a large personal collection of stolen art, mostly from 16th and 17th Century artists.

He stored the artwork in his bedroom at his mother's house in the city of Strasbourg, France. The sight of hundreds of artworks by some of the great masters of the art world must have been a truly great sight to behold.

His method was to visit small galleries and regional museums, where security was lax and the displays not considered to be of great importance to anyone outside of a public viewing space. Most of the time, to avoid any alarms, he would slice out the painting at the edges of the frame.

One of his major hauls was 'Sybille, Princess of Cleves' by Lucas Cranach the Elder. The painting was due to be in a Sotheby's auction and was on display at a castle in Baden-Baden, Germany. The painting was estimated at $7million (USD). He simply sliced it out the frame and walked away.

Prolific

In 1997, two years into the six-year span, Stéphane and Anne-Catherine were arrested when they walked out of a private gallery in Switzerland with a William van Aelst landscape painting. They had been allowed special access to see it by the owner, who believed them to be true art enthusiasts.

The owner followed them to a car where he found a second artwork from another gallery nearby. Stéphane was convicted of theft and given an eight-month suspended sentence and banned from entering Switzerland for three years. Anne-Catherine was cautioned with handling stolen goods.

Stéphane continued working in Switzerland under his mother's maiden name and stole another piece from a gallery near to the one he had been caught at. After his girlfriend split up with him, he went on an art tour of France and in one week was known to have raided a different place every day.

By 2001, Stéphane had accumulated stolen artwork that was worth in excess of $1.5billion (USD), making him the world's most notorious and wealthiest art thief. He was obsessed with exploiting the minimal security of small public spaces across Europe, and for a while was getting away with it.

All across Europe, police in various towns were starting to collate information that many stolen pieces were attributed to just one person and a possible accomplice. In November 2001, Stéphane tried to sell one of the pieces online and it led to his downfall.

Rumbled by a bugle

Stéphane had been able to get away with it for so long as he never sold the artworks, instead keeping them for his own pleasure in his bedroom, despite amassing a huge amount of wealth in asset form.

He stole a 16th Century bugle from a museum in Lucerne, Switzerland, decided he didn't want it, and tried to sell it online for approximately $50,000 (USD). The bugle was only one of three like it in the world, and investigators were keeping an eye on any online movement of the piece.

Before it was sold, Stéphane made the mistake of going back to the same museum two days later, unaware that the guard had clocked him on the way out when he stole the bugle.

A visiting journalist was walking around the museum grounds with his dog when he saw a man in an overcoat acting strangely outside the entrance to the museum. Aware of the recent theft, the journalist informed the guard who recognised Stéphane and immediately apprehended him.

His mother, Marielle Schwengel, had no idea the artwork was stolen, and assumed her son had been collecting small pieces from his travels around Europe. When she heard of her son's arrest for stealing art in Switzerland, she did something that makes art enthusiasts wince to this day.

Destruction of irreplaceable art

It took over two weeks for Swiss authorities to get an international warrant to search Marielle's house in Strasbourg, which gave Marielle the time she needed to help out her son as best she could. Not realising how much the art pieces was worth, she set about destroying them.

Using a pair of scissors and a selection of kitchen knives, she began the process of cutting up the historical artworks and shredding them, under the belief that if there were no paintings or art in her house then there was no proof Stéphane had stolen them.

She left broken parts of frames in trash bags around the city. She also dumped all the vases, jewellery, pottery, statuettes, and ornaments into the Rhone-

Rhine Canal. She had unknowingly destroyed $1.5billion (USD) worth of irreplaceable art.

When investigators got the warrant to search the house, they found no trace of the artwork. It took another four months for Stéphane to finally confess to stealing the items and he managed to list them all in detailed fashion.

Seven months later, some of the more tangible artworks began washing up on the shore of the canal, and Marielle confessed to destroying the artwork but claimed she did so out of anger at her son. One Swiss officer said, '*never have so many old masters been destroyed at the same time*'.

Addicted to art

A team of specialists dragged the bottom of the canal and recovered 110 items but many were damaged beyond repair. Stéphane spent two years in prison in Switzerland before being extradited back to France.

In 2005, he was sentenced by a court in Strasbourg to three more years in prison but served a little over two. There were reports he had become suicidal, and before the French trial had attempted to hang himself but was stopped by a guard.

It turned out that Stéphane had been stealing since he was a child and moving on to bigger and bigger things until he found a fascination with art. Anne-Catherine was sentenced to 18 months and served six, while Marielle was sentenced to three years and served 18 months.

Stéphane wrote an autobiography called '*Confessions of an Art Thief*' published in France in 2006, and

Germany in 2007. But it wasn't the end of his thieving. In 2011, during a house search, police found 30 more artworks, stolen from locations around Europe. He was sentenced to another three years in prison.

In 2019, he was arrested yet again after another search found Roman coins from a museum, and other artworks from galleries in Germany. He was placed under constant surveillance and now has to check in with authorities on regular occasions.

His case publicised the lax security at smaller museums and galleries around Europe and led to better security protocols being implemented. The art world was saddened by the loss of such great works and agreed that a true art connoisseur would have left the art alone to be seen by future generations.

Stéphane Breitwieser remains the most prolific and successful art thief who has ever lived, despite keeping the collections for himself, and only selling off small pieces to keep his collection going strong. At one point, by asset value alone, he was one of the richest men in Europe.

The Muswell Hill Murderer

The sickening tale of British serial killer Dennis Nilsen, who killed 15 young men, and dissected some of their remains – before flushing them down the toilet and blocking the sewers with flesh.

The British Dahmer

Dennis Nilsen is one of Britain's most infamous serial killers. Some see him as the British version of Jeffrey Dahmer, and in a lot of ways, the similarities are striking. They both killed gay men and they made their first kill within five months of each other in 1978. Nilsen killed 15, Dahmer killed 17, and they both carried out necrophilia acts upon the bodies of their victims.

Because of the United Kingdom's different legal system to that of the United States, Dennis Nilsen was sentenced to life, as since 1969, the country no longer carries the death sentence.

Nilsen would request parole hearings for immediate release up until his death in 2018 when he died of natural causes. He reached out from within his cell with now banned autobiographies and interviews to sate the appetite of the curious public.

He murdered 15 young men in London over a five year period and kept the victims' bodies for a certain amount of time after he had killed. Then he dissected them and either burned the remains or flushed them down the toilet.

Viewing the body

During his life, he worked as a military chef, police officer and civil servant. Not the usual career progression to serial killer. To stand in such esteemed positions in work and life and then go on to kill is one that has produced conflicting reports from psychologists and experts alike.

Nilsen was only four-years-old when his parents divorced due to his father's drunkenness, and his mother remarried soon afterwards. The disruption in the British Isles after the dust of World War Two had settled was felt throughout the nation, more so on the children born into that era.

The fallout of World War Two across many countries is considered one of the reasons for the rise of the serial killer in the Seventies and Eighties. For Nilsen, the break-up of his family at a time of national hardship was crippling.

In his trial and subsequent interviews, Nilsen claimed there was an event in his life, at the age of six-years-old, that was to shape him for many years to come. After his mother remarried, she sent him to live with his grandparents.

It was there he found a kinship with his grandfather, Andrew Whyte, but after a couple of years he was returned to his mother. In the Autumn of 1951, Nilsen's grandfather died of a heart attack.

Some serial killers have attributed the death of a grandparent as a turning point in their lives. Alexander Pichushkin, the Russian Chessboard Killer, confirmed that after the death of his grandfather, he turned to vodka, and then to murder.

What didn't help Nilsen's fragile tendencies at the time was that his mother made him view the body of his grandfather due to her strong religious beliefs. Nilsen later stated that the first time he knew of his grandfather's death was when he saw the corpse. He said, '*it caused a sort of emotional death inside me.*'

Relationship with death

Two years later, when he was eight-years-old, Nilsen almost drowned in the seas close to his hometown. An older boy who was on the coast at the time saw what was happening and went in to rescue him.

Nilsen later said that the boy masturbated over his body. He awoke from his experience with near death to find ejaculate on his stomach.

Afterwards, he withdrew into himself, hiding away from the world. He was a loner and kept himself to himself but he was never disliked and had many friends at the time. Yet, he preferred to be with his own company.

He had never killed small animals or exhibited a cruel streak towards living things and was never aggressive or violent towards his peers. He was for all intents and purposes, a good and well-loved child, and the opposite of what a potential serial killer was supposed to have been.

On one occasion he helped in the search of a local man who had gone missing. As fate would have it, it was a young Nilsen and a friend who found the man's body on a riverbank. He later said it had reminded him of seeing the body of his grandfather and upon coming across the corpse he had felt no emotion towards it.

He never had a sexual encounter, nor suffered abuse during his childhood or teenage years. It would be almost two decades later when Nilsen would record his first kill.

The house that death built

He joined the British Army at 17-years-old and stayed there for 11 years. During his time in the military he said he carried with him a huge weight of loneliness. When he was allowed a private room he would lay down in front of a mirror so he couldn't see his own head in the reflection. He would then masturbate to the sight of what he viewed as an unconscious body.

This might in some part have been carried over from his experience on the beach. In 1972 he left the military of his own accord and returned to civilian life. He went on to join the Metropolitan Police in London but only served eight months as an officer before once again leaving of his own accord.

He often witnessed autopsied bodies in close proximity. It fascinated him and he revelled in that part of the work but he left because he felt the job didn't fit him well, having come from the military. In 1974 he went on to work as a civil servant in a job centre in London and became active in trade unions. Then the fantasies he'd long held started to seep into his reality.

There are infamous addresses where killers and murderers have carried out their crimes and lived but none more so than 195 Melrose Avenue. The address in the London area of Cricklewood, would claim 12 victims. He had access to a large garden and was able to burn many of the remains in bonfires. Some of the entrails were thrown over the fence so that local wildlife would consume them.

Nilsen had moved into 195 Melrose Avenue, sometimes listed mistakenly as Melrose Place, with a man named David Gallichan. It was said to have been a purely platonic relationship. Nilsen wanted more however, he wanted real commitment and after a series of casual sexual encounters, his bizarre corpse fantasies started to become more prominent.

When he positioned himself in front of a mirror so that his head appeared as missing, he would start to add fake blood to his corpse to look as though he had been killed. He fantasised someone would take him away and bury him and he started to believe that his corpse was the perfect state of his human body.

There was nothing more emotionally and physically pleasing to him than fantasising about his own dead body. After a rough and stressful relationship with Gallichan, Nilsen forced him to leave but was aware of the consequences of being alone. '*Loneliness*,' he wrote, '*is a long unbearable pain.*'

Limpness of the corpse

A day before New Year's Eve in 1978, Nilsen claimed his first victim, 14-year-old Stephen Holmes, who had been refused alcohol at a local pub. Nilsen took the opportunity to invite him to his flat on Melrose Avenue to drink alcohol with him. '*He was to stay with me over the New Year period whether he wanted to or not.*'

After going to bed together, Nilsen woke at dawn and became aroused at the sight of his new friend's sleeping body. Holmes was sleeping on his front when Nilsen straddled him and slipped a tie under his neck. He subsequently drowned the young boy in a bucket of water by resting his head over the edge of a chair.

After the bubbles stopped rising from the water, Nilsen rested him on the floor realising that he had just killed a man whose name he did not know. He was also suddenly fearful of the consequences of his actions. Again, a trait not carried by most serial killers.

Nilsen said later that he just sat there staring at the boy's fresh corpse, shaking with the fear and stress of the situation. He made himself a coffee and smoked some cigarettes to ease his nerves.

After washing the corpse in the bathroom he returned Holmes to the bed and was fascinated by the limpness of the corpse. *'It was the beginning of the end of my life as I had known it, I had started down the avenue of death and possession of a new kind of flat-mate.'*

Keeping corpses

The concept of keeping corpses as flat-mates was now embedded into Nilsen's psyche. He thought the sight of the corpse was beautiful and not appalling in anyway whatsoever. He hid the body under the floorboards, but after a week had gone by, curiosity had got the better of him – he wanted to see whether the body had changed in anyway.

As he was carrying the body back to the living room, he felt himself becoming aroused and subsequently masturbated onto the corpse's stomach. He even trussed him up by the ankles for an undisclosed amount of time before putting the corpse back under the floorboards.

It would be almost eight months later when Nilsen removed the body to burn it in a bonfire in his garden.

He burned rubber to hide the smell and raked the ashes into his garden. Most of his victims were homeless or homosexual men who he would lure to his home with offers of food, alcohol, or a place to rest their heads.

His victims were normally killed by strangulation or drowning during the course of the night. He then proceeded to use his butchering skills, learned in the British Army, to help him get rid of the bodies.

He would keep them in various different locations around his home but usually under the floorboards and would constantly engage in sexual activity with the corpses.

Over the next three years, Nilsen would murder another 11 men in the ground floor apartment at Melrose Avenue. Of these 11, only four were ever identified.

Kenneth Ockendon was a Canadian tourist he had met at a local pub for lunch in 1979. Nilsen claimed he enjoyed the company of Ockendon and it was the thought of him leaving that drove him to kill again. He strangled him with a headphone cord before washing the body and taking it to bed with him.

Nilsen said he never had sexual intercourse with the corpses but that he did carry out sexual acts with them. He enjoyed masturbating on the corpses and pleasuring himself on certain parts of their bodies. He placed Ockendon under the floorboards and would take the corpse out several times to watch the television with him.

Bodies down the toilet

Nilsen said he would sometimes go into a killing trance and didn't always remember the act of murder. The feeling of control over the corpses of his flat-mates thrilled him and he held a certain fascination with how they deteriorated over time. He believed he was appreciating them more dead than alive.

When the investigation started after Nilsen's arrest, police investigators found over 1000 bone fragments in the garden of 195 Melrose Avenue. He had used the small garden as his own personal burial ground.

Through his butchering career in the British Army he learned the art of butchery so well he would use this skill to rid the house piece by piece of the corpses that remained. He would strip to his underwear and cut them up on the stone floor of his kitchen. He would then place the organs in plastic bags.

His fantasy progressed to removing the head and then heating it in a large pan of water to boil off the flesh of the skull. He would burn the rest of the remains over time, sometimes close to the garden fence. He was constantly amazed that he was never caught or that no one ever questioned him and his strange activities.

Nilsen one day decided to leave Melrose Avenue and move into a new place in the city. In some part to leave the murderous part of his life behind and in others to escape from the torment he had inflicted. Before Fred and Rose West's 25 Cromwell Street was known to the public, 195 Melrose Avenue was the darkest house of horrors in the British Isles.

In 1981, Nilsen moved to 23 Cranley Gardens in Muswell Hill, London, and it proved to be his undoing.

He found it difficult to get rid of the bodies in his new home and ended up with black bin-liners full of human organs in his wardrobe. He would kill three more at Cranley Gardens over the next year and a half.

The last victim was dissected in the same way as the previous ones. The head was boiled and the limbs and organs were placed into bags, ready for disposal. But without access to a garden, Nilsen had to come up with different methods of disposal.

He would boil the flesh off the bones and flush pieces of the bodies down the toilet.

Rotting flesh

One of the other five tenants who lived in the block complained to the landlord the toilet was not flushing properly. Nilsen had apparently tried to clear the blockage with acid and it mostly worked but it didn't clear the blockage in the external drain.

A local plumber called in a specialist team to get a second opinion, and one of the technicians, Michael Cattran, went into the drains beneath the house. He found a gooey sludge blocking a part of the sewer coming from a pipe linked to the property.

It appeared to be various pieces of animal flesh and so he immediately reported it to his superiors. When the sewer team left, Nilsen went down into the sewers and started removing the lumps of flesh that had congealed together. But some of the other tenants noticed his movements and strange actions and reported it to the police.

At the same time, the results came back from the analysis of what was assumed to be animal remains. The results were unquestionable; they were human. Detectives paid a visit to the house the following evening.

End of a disturbing reign

DCI Peter Jay waited at the scene with two officers for Nilsen to return from work, they followed him into the block of flats and they immediately smelled rotting flesh. Nilsen asked why the police were interested in the drains. They told him they had found human remains.

"Good grief, how awful," Nilsen said.

"Don't mess about, son, where's the rest of the body?" DCI Jay responded.

Nilsen remained relaxed and calmly said that the remains of the bodies were in two plastic bags in the wardrobe. When they drove him to the police station, they asked him how many bodies he was actually talking about.

"Fifteen or sixteen since 1978."

He pleaded guilty with diminished responsibility but on November 4th, 1983, he was sentenced to life imprisonment. He was convicted of six murders and two attempted murders. The Home Secretary later imposed a whole life tariff, which meant that he would never be released and would subsequently be denied any requests for parole.

Nilsen died of natural causes in 2018. His disturbing crimes have been made into various movies, TV series, multiple books, and thousands of articles, each trying to uncover the madness behind the eyes of one of Britain's worst serial killers.

The Great Reality TV Swindle

How a down-on-his-luck homeless man conned fame-seeking wannabes to take part in a year-long reality TV show that didn't exist.

The Con

The Great Reality TV Swindle, AKA: Project MS-2, was a con devised and enacted by a British man calling himself Nik Russian. He had placed advertisements in national publications seeking people to audition for a new year-long reality television show for Channel 4 in the UK.

After receiving hundreds of applications from eager fame-seeking reality TV fans, he held auditions at a location called Raven's Ait, which is a small island on the Thames between Surbiton and Kingston, usually used for conferences and weddings.

There, he whittled down the applicants to 30 successful people who would take part. Without telling them that the show hadn't actually been commissioned. He gave them bizarre instructions that many decided didn't add up and left the show before it started.

Russian instructed them to leave their homes, quit their jobs, and meet in London on a specific date in the early Summer of 2002. They signed contracts that meant nothing and left their lives behind for the chance to be on the show.

The Man

Nik Russian was no TV producer, even though he acted like one around the contestants, and managed to charm them into believing a TV show was on the cards. Unfortunately for the contestants on the show, the programme didn't really exist.

He claimed the show was a secret and it went under the name of Project MS-2, to put off curious parties. At the auditions, he had enlisted the help of his friends to be the cameraman, a psychological analyst, and showrunners, all unaware the programme was fake.

Nik Russian wasn't quite who he said he was. Born Keith Anthony Gillard in Surrey in 1977, he went through a series of name changes and personas including Jack Lister and Nikita Russian. He studied English at the University of London, wrote a series of unpublished books, and set up multiple businesses that failed.

By the time he came up with the idea for the show he was working as a customer assistant at the bookstore, Waterstones. When the show went into 'production' on 10th June 2002, Nik left his job, ended the tenancy on his flat, and became literally homeless.

On the 10th of June, the 30 contestants were split into three teams of 10 and instructed to meet at different locations across London. It was only then they discovered what the challenge was.

The Plan

The challenge for the show was to make £1million (GBP) in one year by any means possible as a team. The prize? £100,000 each. Confused by the point of making their own prize money, many of the wannabe TV stars rebelled.

Despite having signed sketchy contracts, the entirety of Team One and Team Three left the show and returned to lives they had temporarily ended. For many, this meant they had to move back in with the parents, having ended relationships and jobs – such was the allure of reality TV fame.

Team Two had no idea the other teams had left the show and were handed their first challenge by the cameraman. The cameraman was Tim Eagle, an eager trainee who had taken on the job for free to gain experience in the industry.

The first task was to find accommodation for free for one week. They also had to find food for free as the production wasn't going to feed them. On that first day in London, many of Team Two were confused by the fact they would be making money themselves that they would keep, but they saw it is a stepping-stone to that all-important fame.

To help them find free accommodation, Tim suggested they could sleep in his house until they found better dwellings. Team Two ended up sleeping on his floor, in the hope that fame and fortune were just around the corner. But something was off and one part of the challenge didn't seem legit.

To ensure the contestants were making money – towards that £1million target, they had to deposit their funds into a bank account owned by Russian, which Russian claimed was to track how much they were making.

The Collapse

After the first night, Team Two were concerned they were being played, and were worried that Tim knew nothing about the programme beyond the fact he had to film them. They decided to use Tim's camera to make their own reality show, while questioning Nik Russian's motives at the same time.

It was at that point that Russian stopped taking phone calls from the team. Some of Team Two left that night but others including Louise Miles, Debbie Driver, and Daniel Pope, remained.

That night, unable to maintain the scam any longer, Russian arrived at Tim's house – as he was homeless – and suggested it was a good idea if he stayed with Team Two. Russian confessed there was no programme commission and the contracts were fake.

On the 12th of June, two days after production had started, Tim contacted the London Tonight news team and said he had a story for them. Aware they had been scammed, the remaining members of Team Two locked Russian in Tim's flat and waited for journalists to arrive.

After answering a few questions, Russian went into hiding and for a while was nowhere to be seen, but a real TV show was on his case. The day after Russian vanished, Debbie contacted two executives, Caz Gorham and Frances Dickenson of indie production company Christmas Television.

When they were told all the details of the swindle, the company decided to produce a special one-off documentary film about what had happened. But of course, they first had to convince the contestants that they were to make a real programme about them, and not a con job.

The Commission

Amazingly, Channel 4, who Russian lied had commissioned the reality TV series, ended up commissioning the documentary from Christmas Television. One of the contestants wasn't sure the documentary was real until a production team turned up with a 'real big camera'.

The aim of the documentary was to expose the swindle and show how the participants were trying to get their lives back together. Realising that Tim the cameraman and other 'production' crew had provided everything for free and were not getting paid, Christmas Television included them in their documentary.

Louise uncovered the truth that Russian's production company didn't even exist, and that the person who took their phone calls in the early days was Russian's mother, Margaret. Daniel tracked down Russian to an address in Richmond and convinced him to be interviewed for the documentary.

The most curious aspect of the story was that Russian believed he had not done anything wrong. He hadn't taken any money from the contestants, nor had he committed a crime, though there were signs that down the line once money started coming in that a crime may have been committed.

He genuinely believed – in the age of reality TV – that his idea for a show would work and that once he presented the series to a production company that it would be purchased and run on TV. But he never got that far, and for many of the contestants, they returned to broken lives, at the tail-end of a confused dream that one man had.

The Collapse

Many had thrown huge going away parties, given away possessions, ended tenancies or sold homes, and some even ended relationships, all for the chance of reality TV success. The official documentary team spent months tracking Russian down, as he moved around a lot within London.

For many of the contestants, though initially feeling sorry for him and his lost dream, pity turned to anger. Many saw him for the conman he was, and that he had psychologically abused many people in order to trick them into earning money for him.

Though he put his own life on the line to make the project work, it remained unforgiveable that he ended up hurting so many people. Many contestants fell into depression and needed a lot of support to get them back into the world.

The documentary was called The Great Reality TV Swindle and was shown on Channel 4 in December 2002. Much of the reaction to the documentary was split. Many placed the blame wholly on Russian for being an unscrupulous conman but some claimed him to be a tragic figure of overstretched ambition.

Some critics – before the heady days of social media – placed the blame squarely on the contestants and the nature of reality TV itself, with The Scotsman newspaper calling them 'gullible wannabes'.

There was an ironic twist for the contestants, that despite the con, it led them to actually appear on TV, not as the wide-eyed eager wannabes in the homemade videos, but as reflective, wounded individuals.

It remains unclear what happened to Russian but with his charming, good looks, and desire to hit the big time, it wouldn't be a surprise if he popped up somewhere else, in another time, with a new name – and a new con.

The Unusual Death of Chuck Morgan

An escrow businessman went missing twice before being found dead, having apparently shot himself in the back of the head, leading to a mystery of organised crime, a secret life, and cover-ups.

Money laundering

For many who knew him, 39-year-old Charles 'Chuck' Morgan, lived a mostly uneventful life. He was a successful businessman in the escrow industry and was married with two daughters. Nothing seemed untoward until the day he came home tied up with a hallucinogenic in his throat.

1970s Arizona was known as one of America's money laundering states, due to a law that allowed land to be purchased using managed money accounts, meaning not belonging to the named person on the account.

For many years, the Mafia were known to have laundered huge amounts of money through Arizona, without as much as raising an eyebrow. They did so without leaving traces of where the money had come from, fundamentally hiding it from anyone who delved deeper.

It was in this industry that Chuck managed to carve out a successful career as an escrow agent, someone who kept large amounts of money, as property or assets were changing hands between two parties. It meant that most likely, Chuck was handling Mafia money, putting his Tucson-based family at risk.

Hallucinogenic

Unknown to many people at the time, Chuck was allegedly working as an agent for the federal government and was supposed to be handing over information about his transactions between various parties. Later on, the government denied any knowledge of Chuck working for them but many believed it was the reason for what happened next.

On 22nd March 1977, Chuck was getting ready to leave for the office, and kissed his wife, Ruth Morgan, goodbye for the day. On the way to work, he dropped off his two daughters at school, but failed to return home that evening, causing Ruth to panic.

Three days later and at two in the morning, Chuck's car crept into the driveway beside the house and caused a nearby dog to start barking, so Ruth ran outside to see who it was. Chuck fell out of the driver's side door and Ruth helped him inside.

Chuck had been tortured but couldn't speak. He was missing a shoe, had a broken handcuff around one ankle – which allowed him to drive – and was tied at the wrists with a plastic zip tie. He grabbed a pen and paper and wrote that he had a hallucinogenic trapped in his throat and it was enough to kill him or drive him crazy if swallowed.

Some reports claim he had the hallucinogen painted onto his throat, but this researcher can find no instance where that method was preferred over forcing someone to swallow a tablet or powder. It remains curious, that if he had a hallucinogen in his throat, that the lining of his throat wouldn't have already absorbed it.

He instructed Ruth to move the car so no-one could see he had returned home. The police were not to be called under any circumstances as a hit would be put out on all the family. Ruth spent an entire week nursing him back to health.

Secret agent and the Bible passage

When he could talk properly again, and the small amount of hallucinogen he had ingested had started to wear off, he told Ruth that he was working as a secret agent for the federal government, with the intention of fighting organised crime.

He claimed his work led him to be directly related to the Mafia and its activities but someone had discovered he was working against them. He had been abducted, taken to a location near the Sky Harbour Airport in Phoenix, and tortured, but managed to escape in the middle of the night.

In the weeks that followed, Chuck returned to work in a limited capacity, and was the only one to drive his daughters to and from school. He wore a bulletproof vest every time he stepped outside. He told his father that if anything happened to him that he had left a letter claiming who would be responsible for his disappearance or death. Sadly, the letter was never found.

Two months later, on 7th June, on the way back from dropping his daughters off at school, Chuck disappeared for a second time. This time, Ruth reported him as a missing person and informed the police.

Nine days passed and Ruth suspected the worst had happened, when she received a phone call from an unidentified female. She said, '*Chuck is fine and everything will be alright.*' She then referred to a Bible passage, '*Ecclesiastes 12, one through eight*', before hanging up the phone.

That specific passage in the King James version of the Bible is too long for it to make sense here, it is included in full after the Bibliography section of this book. The passage basically means someone should always be devoted to God, and that true faith is one that exists all the time, rather than the one that is called upon only when evil is near.

Two days after the phone call, Chuck's body was found in the desert, 30 feet from the highway in San Juan Springs. He had been shot in the back of the head with a bullet from his own .357 Magnum. The gun was lying beside him and it appeared he had taken his own life. But not all was as it seemed.

Unusual code

Chuck was still wearing his bullet proof vest and had died from the single bullet wound to the back of the head. No fingerprints were lifted from his gun but he had gunshot residue on his hand, which was why police ran with the theory he had taken his own life.

There were no fingerprints found anywhere at the death site, which most likely meant Chuck had been killed elsewhere and placed in the desert or moved from the side of the highway. It would have been an awfully difficult suicide to have shot oneself in the back of the head.

An investigation found a note in his pocket with directions to the highway near to where he was found. It was written in his own handwriting. They found his car a bit further down on the side of the highway. Inside they found numerous weapons, ammunition, and a police CB radio.

Pinned inside of his undergarments, they found a $2 bill with curious notes. There were seven Spanish names written in a list with each name beginning with the next in the alphabet from A to G. The bible reference of Ecclesiastes 12, one through eight, was written on the same side.

The reverse of the bill contained in order the first seven names of the men who signed the Declaration of Independence in 1776. Also on the reverse side was a crudely drawn map, leading to a different location between Tucson and Mexico.

Despite a statement from Ruth regarding the first disappearance, and her belief Chuck was murdered, and that the Mafia were most likely responsible, the police concluded that Chuck had in fact taken his own life by shooting himself in the back the head.

Suspicious players

Two days later, an unidentified female called the local police station. She claimed to be the same woman who had spoken to Ruth two days before Chuck was found. She said she had met with him the night before his death at a local motel.

Chuck had been carrying a briefcase full of money, with tens of thousands of dollars inside. The female claimed the money was to pay-off the hitman that the Mafia had hired to kill Chuck. It was his last ditch attempt to turn the tables on the Mafia.

It remained one of the reasons why Chuck had written so many strange things on the $2 bill, and it could have pointed to the identity of the hitman, if indeed it was the hitman who had killed him. It would seem quite a feat for Chuck to have tracked the hitman down, and a bold statement to have attempted to pay him off.

The woman on the phone was never identified but the investigation discovered that Chuck had stayed at the local motel in the two days prior to his death. One of the logical reasons why Chuck didn't contact his wife when he disappeared was that he didn't want to involve her and was hoping upon hope that he would be able to pay off a hitman.

A few weeks after Chuck's death, and despite the police still claiming suicide, two men showed up at Ruth's house, saying they were from the FBI. They wormed they way in and intricately searched the entire house for something they never did find. Ruth checked with the FBI a day later and discovered they had not sent anyone to her home. The identity of the men remains a mystery.

A secret life – and death

As the years passed, and organised crime was being broken apart by law enforcement, it emerged that Chuck had been heavily involved in the money laundering business, and had laundered millions of dollars of assets, rare metals, and cash.

Links were also unearthed with various crime organisations and it materialised that he was a witness for an inquest involving a bank and a case against organised crime. It appeared that Chuck was hiding a secret identity from his family.

In recent years, theories point to the government themselves having a hand in Chuck's murder, and that it *was* murder and not a suicide. If it was the Mafia or big organised crime then they would have simply gone to his home after he escaped and killed him and his family.

If the mob wants someone to disappear, then they make someone disappear. They wouldn't – or haven't in historical data – gone to the extent of placing hallucinogens in someone's throat or painting it onto someone's skin.

The fact he was tortured meant that he had information about something he was not letting on. Was it dark government officials looking for Mafia intel, or was it the other way around? Another theory rests with the alleged hitman.

The hitman approached Chuck and told him to come up with the money to pay him off, gave him a load of fancy clues, then met him in the desert, where the hitman killed him anyway and took off with the money. Or, it was the unidentified female, knowing he had money, who followed him and shot him in the back of the head.

An air of secrecy

There are many mysteries and loose ends to the story of Chuck Morgan, and there is still an air of secrecy and cover-up surrounding it. In 1990, computer graphics worker, Doug Johnston, was shot dead in a parking lot. It was claimed by investigative reporter, Don Deveraux, that the killer was trying to kill him.

Don lived across the street from Johnston's workplace, had a similar look, and a similar car. Don had been investigating the Chuck Morgan case for the Unsolved Mysteries TV show, when Johnston was killed.

In 1991, a writer from Washington named Danny Casolaro was about to provide a private investigator with evidence of Chuck's transactions, when he was mysteriously found dead in a bathtub in a hotel. Both Danny and Don's death were reported as suicide when evidence is to the contrary.

In recent years, one of Chuck's daughters has publicly claimed that her father knew a lot of secrets about Arizona officials but no names emerged. Chuck's death remains a mystery and though listed as a suicide, it remains likely that he was killed.

Ruth died in 2006, with no more knowledge about her husband's life or death. It's certain that he was hiding something from her and the rest of his family, but whatever that was, led to his death, and has seemingly been covered up ever since.

First Human Killed By A Robot

In 1979, one of science fiction's most feared scenarios became reality when Robert Williams became the first person in history to be killed by a robot.

Science fiction

It's one of the age-old bastions of science fiction, that artificial intelligence will one day rise up and turn on its creators. Since the early 20th Century, stories of robots killing humans have become popular, not only as entertainment but as a warning.

On 25th January 1979, in Flat Rock, Michigan, science fiction became science fact, though it was a little less extreme than a Terminator coming after someone. But not so far removed that 25-year-old Robert Williams was killed by a robot.

Robert worked at the Ford Motor Company, at their Flat Rock Casting Plant, a giant manufacturing site. He had been there for a number of years as the job provided decent pay and stability for him and his family.

He was one of three operators of the parts retrieval system where a five-storey robot was sited to retrieve vehicle castings and other parts from high density storage shelves at the plant. It enabled workers to get to the inventory quicker.

When the robot's display showed that the inventory had been miscalculated and the item couldn't be retrieved, Robert was instructed to climb onto the racks to retrieve the part manually. It was there that the robot had other ideas.

Killed by robot

Though we know that the robot was in fact not a sentient being, aware of its surroundings, nor did it malfunction, it did end up killing Robert. As he was reaching for one of the parts on the third level storage rack, the robot arm moved along the rack towards him.

The robot held one-ton transfer boxes, where the mechanical arms would place items in to move inventory around. One of these giant transfer boxes hit Robert in the head from behind and his body was left suspended against the rack.

His body was discovered 30 minutes later by another worker who was becoming concerned about his disappearance. The manufacturing plant was temporarily suspended as the retrieval of the body began, and an investigation carried out.

The robot had been built by Litton Industries, in their Unit Handling Systems Division. They had built numerous similar machines for various sites across the United States. It was Litton who came under fire for the death.

Not enough safety measures

Robert's family sued the robot manufacturer and alleged that 'Litton was negligent in designing, manufacturing and supplying the storage system and in failing to warn operators of foreseeable dangers in working within the storage area.'

Four years after Robert was killed, a court awarded a landmark $10million (USD) to his family and concluded the trial by stating that Litton had not built in enough safety measures to their system, and that if the system wasn't changed there could have been more deaths.

The award was raised to $15million but Litton settled an undisclosed amount to Robert's family, as a deal for the company not having to admit negligence, which would have resulted in an even higher fine and higher penalties.

Litton Industries then tried to sue Ford, claiming they hadn't sent Robert to Litton-approved safety training but a judge threw out the case before it got to trial, citing the evidence that it was the machinery that was unsafe and not the plant where it was installed by Litton.

Though we might not see the mechanical arm as a robot of science fiction, it was a robot nonetheless, and since 1979, robotics have increased to such a level that every segment of industry uses them.

Today's robots do everything from protect elderly people, vacuum floors, harvest food, travel to other planets as roving vehicles, create computer parts, carry out attacks as part of drone systems, and even control every aspect of our homes.

In 1979, the concept of any of those becoming reality was science fiction, and the Litton retrieval system was as high-tech as it got.

Increase in robot-related incidents

Later, the director of the Mobile Robot Laboratory in Georgia, claimed that the death was an industrial accident, which led some theorists to conclude that the robot arm was able to detect human presence, and as such had ignored its protocols to kill Robert.

Regardless of the wild theories, the machine did not have the safety measures in place and Robert was killed by the robot, unintentionally. The real crime here was committed by Litton who simply didn't have the safety measures in place to stop an accident like it, and they were fined accordingly.

In today's world, artificial intelligence is so advanced that scientists are exploring the possibility that robots or other sentient beings will soon need to have their own lawyers. This is being explored due to the fact that one day soon, our Alexa or Echo devices will become real robot companions for humans, along with driverless automatic vehicles to get us around.

For Robert Williams, he would go down in history as the first person to have been killed by a robot. His family, though bolstered by a large pay-out, still lost their loved one, and it should have sent a shockwave through the robotics industry. But it didn't.

Each year, with the increase in technology, tens of thousands of people across the world become involved in robot-related incidents. It's perhaps a grim realisation that Robert's death was not only the first death by robot, but the first in a long and ever-growing list.

Satanic Murder of Arlis Perry

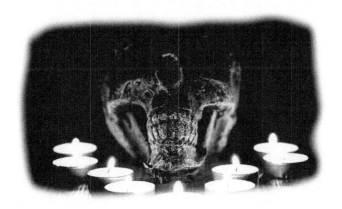

A young newlywed went to church to pray and fell victim to an evil killer who did unspeakable things to her body. The killer got away with it for almost half a century until he was finally revealed.

Fear of Satanism

Everyone was against Satanism in the Seventies and Eighties, none more so than the newspapers, who had instilled the notion of Satanic Panic. The fear of Satanism, and occultism to some degree, was only bolstered by the occasional murder that appeared to be ritualistic.

Perhaps no more so than the ritualistic murder of 19-year-old Arlis Perry on 12th October 1974 in California. Fortunately for Arlis, unlike many other murders of the era, a cold case investigation was able to solve it after 44 years.

At the time, the case was linked to Satanists, cults, gangs, serial killers, and the Son of Sam murderer; David Berkowitz, who expressed that he knew more about the murder than the police themselves.

For almost half a century, Arlis' case was one of the most infamous in relation to possible Satanic ritual, and when you read on how she had come to meet her fate, you might just realise why. For her death and desecration of her body was nothing if not born out of absolute evil.

Evil was afoot

Born Arlis Kay Dykema in Bismarck, North Dakota, she was raised in a deeply religious family, and carried on the religious trend throughout her teenage years. The love of her life was Bruce D. Perry, and they had been infatuated with each other since high school.

In August 1974, six weeks before her death, the high school sweethearts married at a small ceremony in North Dakota. Bruce, who was a sophomore pre-med student, was going to study in California, and the couple moved there within days of being married.

They moved into Quillen Hall on the Stanford University campus, and Arlis managed to find work as a receptionist at a local law firm. With a new job, and a new marriage, the couple had already started planning for their future. But evil was afoot in the grounds of Stanford University.

Just before midnight on 12th October, the young couple argued over the tyre pressure on their car. Feeling stressed about the situation, Arlis wanted to go and pray alone at the Stanford Memorial Church, which was an iconic landmark on the University campus.

At around 3am, Bruce became worried that Arlis hadn't returned home, and called the police. Shortly after, officers went to the church to check on Arlis but found the doors to the building were locked, and there were no signs of life inside.

One of the campus security guards, and former police officer, Stephen Black Crawford, said he locked the church at around midnight, the time when Arlis had supposedly gone there. He also did a check of the church at 2am, as was common with the nightshift routine.

When Crawford went to the church at 5.45am to open it for the early morning mass, he stumbled upon Arlis' body.

Ritualistic murder

In the east transept of the cross-shaped church, and near the altar, was the partially nude body of Arlis. She was lying on her back with her face turned up to the roof. Embedded in the back of her head was an ice pick, which had been broken off from the handle, due to the force of the attack.

A one-metre tall altar candle had been forcibly pushed into her vagina, and another same-sized candle was rested in-between her breasts. Her jeans had been arranged on her legs in a diamond shape pattern. She also had neck injuries consistent with violent strangulation.

Crawford said he had found the west side door open and it had been forced from the inside, which led investigators to suspect the killer or killers were inside the church when Crawford was performing his early morning checks of the perimeter.

Immediately, both Bruce and Crawford became suspects. Investigators found semen on a pillow next to Arlis' body, and a partial palm print on one of the candles. Both pieces of evidence didn't match the pair, and they were removed from the suspect list.

Detectives at the time initially linked the bizarre murder to three previous ones in the same area, that had occurred in the previous year. Those murders were later attributed to American serial killer John Arthur Getreu, who was arrested in 2018 and sentenced to life in prison.

But for a while, the Arlis murder had everyone stumped. The ritualistic style of her death led some officers to consider that Satanic groups were involved, even though there is no known ritual in occultism or elsewhere involving the insertion of a candle into a vagina.

Son of Sam

Detectives discovered that seven people had been in the church on the 12th of October, including Bruce and Crawford, who along with four others were ruled out. A seventh person remained unidentified but a passing witness came forward to claim that he saw a man trying to enter the church around midnight.

The witness said the man had sandy-coloured hair, was of medium build, and was not wearing a watch, which was a bizarre thing to notice. Despite the brutal nature of the murder and display of the body, the Arlis case went cold.

Five years later, serial killer David Berkowitz, AKA: The Son of Sam, wrote about the Arlis murder in a number of letters which were picked up the San Jose Mercury News team. In it, he claimed that the alleged culprit of the Arlis murder was someone he referred to as 'Manson II'.

Investigative journalist, Maury Terry, had become convinced that David Berkowitz, who killed six people and injured nine, did not act alone. The theory goes that Berkowitz was part of a Satanic cult involving at least three other members, and that Manson II was a codename for one of the individuals in that group.

One theory rested on the belief that Arlis was aware of a cult in the area and had gone to the church that night, in an attempt to convert them back to Christianity and its values. But the investigation could find no link between Satanism or Berkowitz.

As the years went by, a retired Santa Clara Police detective, Ken Kahn, theorised that Crawford had locked Arlis into the church by mistake, along with another unidentified person. That person then crept up on Arlis and killed her before breaking out through the west side door.

Yet, the ritualistic style of the murder was not lost on researchers down the years. The case went cold until 2018 when advancements in DNA technology and genetic genealogy testing revealed the true identity of the killer, someone who had been hiding in plain sight.

Hiding in plain sight

In 2018, after confirming DNA evidence they had on record, police went to a San Jose apartment with a search and arrest warrant. The apartment belonged to the then 72-year-old security guard, Stephen Crawford.

He had managed to keep police off his scent from just a few hours after the murder and had maintained his secret for almost half a century. When police arrived at the property, Crawford locked himself in, got hold of his gun, and shot himself in the head, dying of his wound immediately.

Police had always suspected Crawford, due to the timescales of when he performed his checks but they needed advancements in DNA technology to prove it.

The breakthrough came when Arlis' clothes were retested for DNA, and it matched that of Crawford's.

Crawford had gone into the church when Arlis was praying and stabbed her in the back of the head with the ice pick before doing things to her body that the first officers on the scene would never forget. It was suspected he did so as an opportunistic act but also out of his hatred for the University.

Despite knowing who killed Arlis, the connection to David Berkowitz remains, as in Crawford's apartment were numerous books about the occult and the Son of Sam, leading some researchers to suspect that Crawford was part of the same secret Satanic cult as Berkowitz.

For 88-year-old Jean Dykema, Arlis' mother, she was shocked and yet relieved that her daughter's killer had finally been revealed, despite the killer not facing justice.

For Arlis' father, he had passed away only three months before Crawford was identified and went to the grave not knowing who had really killed his daughter.

Whether the Satanic Panic of the Seventies and Eighties was a smokescreen or a legitimate epidemic, it remains clear that many feared it was real. Crawford may have been trying to emulate the darkness that Satanism evoked. Or maybe he was a Berkowitz fanatic who chose to kill when the opportunity presented itself.

As for Arlis, her case was closed almost half a century after her death, bringing hope to all the other families waiting for justice in the annals of historical true crime. Waiting for that same knock on the door to tell them their loved one's killer has finally been found.

Reincarnation of Two Murdered Girls

A year after two sisters were killed in a hit-and-run, their parents gave birth to twin girls, and claimed they were the reincarnated souls of the sisters, in one of the most convincing cases of reincarnation.

The Pollocks

The town of Hexham, in Northumberland, England, is known predominantly for its Anglo-Saxon history, the Hexham Abbey, and its proximity to Hadrian's wall, the former Roman boundary between Roman Britannia, and Caledonia (Scotland) in the North.

For modern mystery and true crime enthusiasts, Hexham is known for the murder of the Pollock sisters, and their alleged reincarnation as twin girls to the same parents. John Pollock was born in Bristol in 1920, and met the love of his life, Joanna Pollock, in the same area.

Both were devout Catholics, with Florence carrying on the work of God at the Salvation Army in the city. Their third child and first daughter, Joanna Pollock, was born in 1946, and shortly after they moved to Hexham.

Their second daughter, Jacqueline, was born in 1951. John and Florence were busy with their new grocery and milk delivery business they had created, and so the two girls were mostly raised by their maternal grandmother.

In May of 1957, Joanna, 11, and Jacqueline, 6, were walking to church with their friend, Anthony, 9, when a nearby car revved up and purposely sped towards them.

It crashed into them, killing both girls instantly, and leaving Anthony fighting for his life, only to die in hospital the next day.

Grief

A hit-and-run is bad enough but it had been no accident. The female driver, who has never been named, was a Hexham local who had recently been forcibly separated from her own children. She swallowed a large amount of prescription drugs then got into her car.

She erratically drove around town with the sole intention of killing herself and any children, out of revenge for hers being taken away. Witnesses to the crash watched in horror as the three children, trapped by a wall, were thrown into the air like ragdolls.

The woman managed to drive to the next road over, when the impact of the crash stopped the engine. Nearby pedestrians held her until police arrived. She was ultimately admitted to a psychiatric hospital, and there remains little information as to what happened to her.

Understandably, both John and Florence fell into a deep depression that showed no signs of improving. As they grieved, and national press jumped on the story, they shared details of the girl's lives.

Eerily, Joanna often claimed to her father that she would never grow up to be a lady, which was a chilling premonition of her death. Jacqueline had been born with a birthmark on her left wrist and had a scar above her right eye after an accident when she was three.

Less than a year later, Florence became pregnant again, and John became convinced they were about to give birth to twin girls, who would be the reincarnated souls of their dead daughters.

Reincarnation

Florence didn't agree with John's beliefs and the twin theory was debunked by their doctor who detected only one heartbeat. The doctor also said it was extremely unlikely they would give birth to twins as no-one in their family had twins, nor was there any medical sign Florence was to have any.

In October 1958, Florence gave birth to – twins. The two girls were named Gillian and Jennifer. Despite being identical twins, the girls had different birthmarks. To their shock, the Pollock's discovered that Jennifer had two birthmarks, one on her left wrist, and one above her right eye, matching the birthmark and scar of Jacqueline.

When the girls were three-months-old, the family moved to Whitley Bay, 30 miles east of Hexham, where John and Florence restarted their business. It was there, they began to notice unusual traits that mimicked the personalities of their dead daughters.

Florence was still angry at John, as she believed he had prayed for Joanna and Jacqueline to be reincarnated before the girls had been killed, and that Gillian and Jennifer were the result of his prayers to God, and belief in reincarnation.

When the girls were three, they were able to identify toys belonging to Joanna and Jacqueline and separated them. Gillian claimed ownership of the toys that had belonged to Joanna, and Jennifer kept the toys that had belonged to Jacqueline.

Creepily, they referred to the toys with the same names as the deceased girls used. They also knew which toys had come from 'Santa Claus' and which had been gifted to them by their parents.

The blood is coming out the eyes

When the twins were four, the family took a day trip to Hexham, which led to more surprises. Without having ever visited Hexham, the girls were able to point out landmarks, knew where the school was that Joanna and Jacqueline had attended, and knew their way to the swings in a public park, as if they had been there before.

Still unconvinced, Florence continued to reject John's belief that the twins were the reincarnated souls of their dead daughters. That was until she overheard the two girls talking about the murder of their dead sisters.

When the girls were four, Florence was standing outside their bedroom as they played a game. She watched Gillian holding Jennifer's head and heard her say; *'the blood is coming out of your eyes. That is where the car hit you'*.

The two girls were known to have recreated the car crash on numerous occasions, with details that their parents confirmed they had never mentioned. Gillian also seemed to know that the birthmark on Jennifer's head was in the same location where Jacqueline hit her head aged three.

Whenever they were outside, the twins had a fear of cars, and when a car revved its engine, they would cling to each other in fear. Jennifer was once heard saying; *'the car is coming to get us and take us away.'*

Reincarnation researcher

At the same time Florence started to believe that reincarnation was possible, a researcher named Ian Stevenson, who had read of the story in the newspapers, contacted the Pollocks to arrange a meeting with the twins.

Known for his research into reincarnation, Ian interviewed the parents and twins at great length, noting birthmarks, stories, and memories of the past. No findings were published initially but he met them again in 1967 and then in 1978 when the twins were twenty.

Blood tests taken in 1978 showed they were identical twins, which normally meant the birthmarks would be in the same place, but they weren't. After Florence's death in 1979, and John's in 1985, Ian published a detailed case report on the possibility of the twins reincarnation.

It detailed in great length how the twins talked about the car accident in the present tense, as if they were reliving it each time. The report also detailed similarities in personality between the twins and the two deceased girls.

Ian was an unbiased researcher but was a researcher into reincarnation, nonetheless. He worked on 895 cases of reincarnation, with 14 cases closer to proof of reincarnation than any others. The Pollock sisters were included in that list of 14.

But Ian concluded that any reincarnation evidence is likely linked to influences in childhood. Despite the Pollock twins begin touted as proof of reincarnation, many have argued against it, and claimed that John specifically had embedded that idea into his children.

Parental Impression

Florence and John claimed they never spoke to the girls about their dead sisters until they were much older, but it's likely the twins may have learnt the story of Joanna and Jacqueline through their older brothers.

It's also not uncommon for young children to pick up on the stresses of their parents, and as Florence and John were still grieving, it's likely they projected their grief onto the twins. They would also have been fearful of cars and talked about Hexham a lot before the visit there.

Later on in life, the adult twins simply accepted their parents beliefs they were the reincarnated souls of their sisters but were sceptical about the notion of reincarnation in general. They claimed to have no memory of any previous life.

Ian later claimed that the case was 'evidentially weak' due to the only witnesses being the parents, and the death of the girls being talked about by them and other relatives while the twins were growing up. A journalist later claimed that if John had not believed in reincarnation, then there would have been nothing to report.

However, Ian later wrote that genetics could not explain Jennifer's birthmark and found it inconceivable that John or Florence could have moulded the twins behaviours to match that of their dead daughters.

Reincarnation or parental impression? Mystery or explainable? Wherever we lay on the spectrum, it remains difficult to imagine how psychologically damaging the murder of children is to the parents who experience it.

Whether the parents instilled their beliefs into the twins, or whether the twins were indeed the reincarnated souls of their sisters, comes down to your belief as to whether reincarnation exists, or not.

Killer In the Walls

A creepy intruder terrorised a family by living in the walls of their home and making them think the house was haunted, in a true urban legend that ended with multiple murder.

The Andrews

Many horror stories flip the notion that a home should be safe and protected and turn it into a place of nightmarish terror and fear. Horror turns home security on its head by giving us haunted houses, poltergeists, home invasions, and secrets in the basement.

Like many great stories, most are based on some elements of truth, and none more so than the killer who hid in the walls of a family home and made them believe it was haunted. Giving us a haunted house and invasion tale in one.

In Townsend, Massachusetts, in 1986, 16-year-old schoolgirl Annie Andrews was excited to be going on a blind date with a guy she had spoken to on the phone. Her life had been going downhill, with her mother dying of cancer just a few months earlier.

She lived with her father, Brian, and younger sister, Jessica, in a large house on the far side of town. Out of the blue, Annie received a phone call from a teenage boy named Daniel LaPlante. He said he got her number from some friends and that they went to the same school together.

Daniel described himself as tall, blond, athletic, and handsome, and lived close by. Taken by his charm, Annie agreed to go on a date with him, except, when they met, Daniel wasn't quite what he claimed to be.

Forged in violence and abuse

She had made the mistake of inviting him over to her house, but when she opened the door, she saw that

Daniel had greasy black hair and was wearing dirty clothes. He wasn't athletic, and Annie agreed with herself that he wasn't handsome. Still, she decided to go on the date with him.

They went into town and had some ice cream from a local café, which was the best part of the date, because everything else was horrible. Daniel was insistent that Annie talked to him about her recently dead mother and began asking inappropriate questions about her sexuality.

Annie quickly ended the date and refused to answer any more phone calls from him, but she was a little fearful that Daniel knew where she lived. Unknown to Annie, Daniel wasn't quite finished with her.

Daniel was born in 1970 to a violent father who beat and sexually abused him throughout his formative years. It was later confirmed that Daniel had also been abused by many family friends around the same time.

Unsurprisingly, the abuse affected every aspect of his life and he struggled academically and socially. He had no friends, was an outcast at school, and was often described as the weird one. The school sent him to a psychiatrist who diagnosed him with multiple disorders.

It was with unfortunate hindsight that the psychiatrist would also abuse Daniel and make him perform sexual acts. It seemed wherever Daniel went, he was losing his grip on humanity. Until he became infatuated with Annie.

The haunting

Due to the recent loss of their mother, Annie and Jessica decided to hold a séance in the basement of their home. They wanted to try and reach out to their mother and tell her how much they loved her. Although nothing strange happened during the séance, what happened after was freaky.

That same night, while in their beds, both girls heard a mysterious knocking and concluded they had invoked an evil spirit. They asked questions to the spirit and were shocked when it answered by tapping on the walls. But it didn't end there.

The knocking on the walls continued at all hours of the day and night and was beginning to freak the sisters out. They told their father, Brian, who laughed it off and said they were making it all up, and that they should never mess with the ways of the occult.

In the days and weeks that followed the séance, more strange things started happening. Sometimes, the furniture had been moved into different positions, and items from the kitchen were found in different parts of the house.

Items they placed on the dining table were later found on the floor beside the table, displayed in an unusual manner. The knocking also continued in various parts of the house, and also when the girls would shower.

They also found written signs on mirrors, and their undergarments moved from drawer to drawer. Still, Brian didn't believe them and put it down to the loss of their mother affecting them. Then, after finding a note in their bedroom that read, *'I'm back, find me if you can,*' and words written in blood on the basement wall, the sisters ran screaming from the house.

Descent into murder

While at work, Brian received word from his neighbours that his daughters were with them. He returned home to find the words in the basement had been written with ketchup and not blood. When he went upstairs to the bedroom, he found Daniel, dressed up in the clothes of his deceased wife.

They got into a fight but Daniel managed to escape and disappear, seemingly into thin air. When police searched the house, they found a hidden section behind Annie's closet. When they went inside, they found Daniel hiding in the walls of the house.

An investigation discovered that Daniel had been hiding in the walls and crawlspace of the house for many weeks and had made peepholes into the walls to spy on the family, even in the bathroom, and the girl's bedrooms.

Daniel was only sentenced to a few months in juvenile detention for trespassing and inciting fear. He was out on the streets within a couple of months and began stealing from shops and houses. On one of his raids, he stole two guns.

On 1st December 1987, during the day, he broke into the Gustafson household, only a mile from Annie's house. He stumbled across 33-year-old pregnant mother Priscilla Gustafson and her two children, seven-year-old Abigail and five-year-old William.

Daniel raped Priscilla in front of her children then shot her at point blank range in the head. He then strangled Abigail, hit her over the head, and drowned her face-down in the downstairs bathtub. He drowned William in the upstairs bathtub.

Andrew Gustafson returned home at 5pm and discovered his family had been slaughtered, including his unborn baby.

Urban legend

It didn't take long for investigators to link Daniel to the murders. There was a lot of genetic evidence left at the crime scene, and many of the stolen items were found in a search of Daniel's family home. He was arrested and quickly sent to trial.

In 1988, 18-year-old Daniel was sentenced to three consecutive life sentences for the murders of the Gustafson family. There was no death penalty in Massachusetts at the time, and life without parole was the maximum penalty available.

In 2013, Daniel allegedly became a Wiccan and tried to sue the state of Massachusetts for not allowing him access to various items to practice the modern Pagan religion. He failed. In a 2017 parole hearing, he was resentenced due to a psychiatrist's report that stated Daniel showed no remorse.

A 2019 parole hearing, held due to a change in sentences relating to crimes committed by minors, upheld the sentences, meaning that Daniel is unlikely to ever be released into the community.

His crimes as a teenager are as horrific as they are creepy, forged in the hell of child abuse, he inflicted that pain upon others. The next time you hear knocking on the walls, it might not be that ghostly spirit you invoked, but the creepy urban legend of someone living in the walls of your home.

Bodies in the Barrels

In Snowtown, a master manipulator convinced others to help him commit serial murder and dispose of their victims' bodies in barrels of acid, leaving 12 dead, and a town forever tainted by infamy.

The Snowtown Murders

Before 1999, Snowtown in Adelaide, Australia, was known for its location on the main road and rail routes between Adelaide and Perth. With a population of a little under 500, the region relied on its crop economy and nearby salt mine.

That all changed when the town became the location where the remains of eight bodies were found in barrels of acid kept in a disused bank vault. Though only one of the murders took place there, Snowtown quickly found itself becoming a hub for true crime enthusiasts and dark tourism.

Between 1992 and 1999, John Bunting, Robert Wagner and James Vlassakis killed at least 12 people between them. A fourth member, Mark Haydon, was convicted on conspiracy to murder as he had helped dispose of the bodies.

Each of the victims had been dismembered and left to rot. Most of the victims were the killer's own family members or acquaintances that one of them knew. The discovery and resulting trial made Snowtown famous for all the wrong reasons.

The Snowtown Murders, more commonly known as the Bodies in the Barrels, are one of the most infamous cases in Australian history, a series of killings carried out by three serial killers, operating as part of a gang.

Rock spider

John Bunting, born in 1966 Queensland, claimed that each of the victims were either paedophiles, gay men, or simply considered inferior, traits that angered him. He made the others believe that murder was the right way to do things, to rid the world of true evil, as he saw it.

Before they killed their victims, they subjected each of them to horrific torture. All the victim's identities were stolen, and their bank accounts were emptied. Bunting was the ring-leader of the serial killing gang and instigated all of the murders.

When he was eight-years-old, he was violently beaten and raped by one of his friend's family members. The abuse he received was linked to him wishing to kill those who attacked children, and he made it his life's mission.

In Australia, the slang for a paedophile is rock spider. In one of the rooms of his home, Bunting created a rock spider wall of information, where he stuck the names and photos of people he suspected to be paedophiles or gay men.

He bundled gay men under the same rock spider banner, as he saw them as immoral and dirty, and linked to child abuse. He had managed to convince himself that gay men were as bad as child abusers, and that any men who showed weakness should be punished.

Bunting was known to be socially active and easy to talk to, this allowed him to bring people in close and manipulate others. This gave him a level of control over others who wanted to help him out or do things for him, but his darker side would shine through more often than not.

When he was in his early twenties, he worked at an abattoir and bragged to his friends and family about how he could skin and slice up any animal with ease. His love of butchery carried over into his everyday life.

He once killed a friend's dog simply because he wanted to see how the body functioned, claiming he was curious about the anatomy of animals and humans. He also told others that he skinned cats alive and enjoyed slaughtering animals whenever he found the opportunity.

Manipulation

In 1991, Bunting and his new wife moved to North Salisbury in South Australia, where his animal killings escalated into human murder. The first murder took place in 1992.

Bunting invited 20-year-old Clinton Trezise over for a drink at his place and accused him of being a paedophile. After a fiery argument, Bunting beat Trezise to death with a shovel, and buried the body in a shallow grave, it was a murder that paved the way for Bunting to claim more lives.

Clinton's body was discovered two years later in 1994 near the tiny town of Lower Light, but due to the decomposition, there was little evidence to suggest how he had died or who had killed him. It was later never proven that Clinton was a child abuser.

His was one of two bodies not found in the barrels or in Bunting's garden. The other was Thomas Trevilyan, who was found on the same day he had been killed in November 1997, again with little evidence pointing to a suspect.

It led many later researchers to suggest that Bunting would use the paedophile or gay angle as an excuse to kill, and as a lure for the other men he roped into killing.

Bunting's neighbour, Robert Joe Wagner, was befriended by Bunting in 1991, and was encouraged to take part in the murders from 1995. At first, Robert thought he was helping as a vigilante but as time went on, Bunting's murders became less focused, and incredibly violent.

Wagner had just ended a relationship with Vanessa Lane, a transgender woman with a history of paedophilia. Formerly Barry Lane, they had started their relationship when Robert was only 14. The age gap was something that later enraged Bunting.

Bunting was married to Elizabeth Harvey, who had a son from a different marriage named James Vlassakis. He convinced James to help him kill those who deserved it, and James also went on to suggest victims. It was later discovered that Elizabeth assisted in at least one of the murders.

Mark Haydon lived near to the Bunting household, and he too was befriended by Bunting, and brought into his circle of killers and torturers. Haydon's cousin, Jodie Elliott, also helped out with claiming insurance and welfare benefits. With the gang growing in size, the murders escalated.

The next murder was in December 1995, when 26-year-old Ray Davies was tortured and murdered. A full victim list along with their statistics is available after the bibliography at the end of this book.

Torturous cannibals

Many victims were subjected to horrific torture. This included knives, ropes, gloves, pliers, a shotgun, metal rods and an electric shock tool, which was used on the genitals of the men they killed.

On some of their victims, they crushed the toes with pliers, shoved lit sparklers into their genitals, burned their ears and nose with cigarettes, and beat them with clubs and metal rods. The killers ordered their victims to refer to them by many controlling names, including Master, God, or Lord.

Some of the victims were killed in their own homes, and the gang would rampage through their houses, smashing things up before killing them. They would also trash the homes of other people they believed to be gay.

Most victims however were lured to Bunting's home, where they were tortured before being dismembered. One of these was Vanessa Lane, Robert's ex-partner, who they decided deserved to be killed for having involved herself with Robert at such a young age.

It was Robert who instigated much of the torture on her. Lane's new partner, Thomas Trevilyan, who was part of the group for a short while, was also killed just weeks after Lane in 1997. One of Bunting's ex-girlfriend's was also killed, along with Elizabeth Haydon, Mark's wife. Many of the gang ended up killing members of their own family.

The group also tortured and killed James' friend, his half-brother, and the final victim, James' stepbrother, David Johnson. By this point, the group had rented a disused bank building in Snowtown. To hide the remains of their victims, they stored them in barrels full of acid, which they moved around to avoid detection.

James had lured the final victim to the bank building where the others were waiting. They tied him down and told him to read from a pre-written script, which included fake crimes and false confessions of things that Johnson had never done. They went to empty Johnson's bank account from an ATM and when they returned, he had died from his injuries.

This upset Robert, who claimed they hadn't made the most of their time torturing him. To appease him, everyone helped dismember Johnson's body and sliced off parts of his flesh, then they fried the body parts and sat down to feast on Johnson's remains.

Rotting very nicely

Eight of the bodies were found in giant plastic barrels that were full of acid. Two of the bodies had been pushed into just one of the barrels. They stored the barrels in the old bank vault, and Bunting would return to them on regular occasions to see how well they were being dissolved in the acid.

Bunting said, 'they're rotting very nicely,' when remarking on the first victim to be put in a barrel. He enjoyed watching the bodies dissolve and made notes on how long it took each body part to rot away.

Though David was the last victim, the group were ultimately caught as a result of the investigation into the disappearance of Mark's wife, Elizabeth Haydon. She had been killed because Bunting claimed she had made sexual advances towards him and he saw this as immoral and dirty – thus she needed to die.

She was killed without Mark knowing about it. When he was shown the body in the barrel, Mark reportedly huffed and smiled to himself. Enquiries into Elizabeth's disappearance ultimately led investigators to the old bank where they found the barrels.

Police suspected the group moved the barrels around to avoid detection, mostly because they knew they were being investigated. When police searched Bunting's home, they found two more bodies buried in his garden.

On 21st of May 1999, Bunting, Robert, James, and Mark were arrested on suspicion of murder. The subsequent trials were among the lengthiest and most expensive in Australian history.

Bunting showed no remorse for his crimes and spoke about the torture of the victims in such an open manner that three of the jury members walked out with their hands over their mouths. He also ignored the proceedings, instead reading a book, and refusing to listen to what was going on around him.

Infamy

They were all sentenced in 2003. Bunting received 11 life sentences without the possibility of parole, for the murders of 11 people. The body of his ex-girlfriend, Suzanne Allen, who was killed in 1996, was found shortly after the barrels were discovered.

Due to her case being tried beforehand with suspects who were innocent, it was decided not to try her case again due to the agreed conclusion that Bunting had killed her, and that it wouldn't affect his overall sentence. Hence why Bunting was convicted of 11 murders and not 12.

Robert got life without the possibility of parole for his participation in nine murders. For his involvement in the crimes, Jamie was sentenced to life with a 26-year minimum term, after striking a plea deal to testify against Bunting and Robert.

Mark got 25 years in jail with a minimum term of 18 years. He struck a plea deal where he would not be charged with murder, but for helping the group of serial killers dispose of some of the bodies. Other people involved who helped in some way, struck plea deals to testify against Bunting.

It's not uncommon to read about serial killing couples or pairs, but rarer to find a case about a gang of serial killers. Bunting was at the heart of the mission to destroy gays, paedophiles, and weak men, and he was able to manipulate other men into killing as part of his mission.

Snowtown is now synonymous with the murders, and at one point, the community had voted to change the name to Rosetown, but for whatever reason, it didn't happen. However, the murders gained such infamy that tourist shops in the area began selling Snowtown murder souvenirs.

The rise of dark tourism and true crime enthusiasm meant that some shops in Snowtown never stopped selling bizarre souvenirs related to the murders. With the salt mine and crop industry giving diminishing returns, the dark tourism one unexpectedly took off, and solidified Snowtown's place in true crime infamy.

The Bennington Triangle Disappearances

At least 40 people have mysteriously disappeared in and around an abandoned town, where eerie and unexplained events happen, along with the curse of a nearby mountain said to swallow its victims.

Glastenbury Mountain

Bennington County in Vermont is the oldest county in the state, created by its first general assembly way back in 1778. The large county is populated by less than 40,000 people, which over the years has led to many towns being abandoned or becoming unincorporated.

Two of these towns, which due to low populations have no government, are Somerset and Glastenbury, spelt with an 'e' and not as its namesake, Glastonbury in England, which is in the county of Somerset – ah, history!

Glastenbury has a population of nine, and somerset a population of six. Other towns nearby where disappearances have been recorded are Shaftsbury, Woodford, and Bennington town itself, with a population of over 15,000.

Many of these towns are gateways to Glastenbury Mountain, standing almost 4,000 feet (1,200 metres) high, and part of the Green Mountain National Forest. It is the mountain that has since become a focal point, not only for hikers, but for a series of strange murders and disappearances.

While some people suspect a mountain-based serial killer, or one who lives in one of the abandoned towns, others believe that supernatural or paranormal activity is behind the disappearances. In a combined area known as the Bennington Triangle, an estimated 40 people have vanished without a trace over a period of 70 years, with curses stretching back centuries.

Bennington Triangle

Bennington Triangle was a phrase created by New England author, Joseph Citro, and was first heard on a radio show in 1992. The loosely-defined triangle mapped out an area of Bennington County, including Glastenbury Mountain where five people had gone missing between 1945 and 1950.

Though the author's focus was on the five missing people, researchers and new developments have showed that over 40 people have disappeared within the triangle. The first to be noted was 74-year-old Middie Rivers who vanished as he was guiding a group of hunters in 1945.

On the return leg, he went ahead of the group and was never seen again, alive or dead. A 300-strong search and rescue team found an unused rifle cartridge in a nearby stream that belonged to Middie, but no other evidence was uncovered. He, like most of the others in time, had simply disappeared off the earth.

Like Middie, 18-year-old Paula Welden was an experienced hiker who vanished a year later on 1st December 1946 while hiking the Long Trail through Vermont, which took in the Glastenbury Mountain. She had worked two shifts in the Commons room at Bennington College before changing her clothes and getting ready for a hike.

A Bennington local helped her with directions, and she passed an elderly couple and many other students on the trail. The FBI became involved when Paula did not return to her college campus in the town.

When agents interviewed the couple, they claimed that Paula had walked past them and turned a corner up ahead. When they reached the corner of the trail less than a minute later, Paula had vanished, with no sign of where she had gone to. Other students backed up the route she had taken and pinpointed sightings of her on the trail.

Her roommate said that Paula was depressed due to being homesick and wanted to go home to see her parents, but she wanted to visit Everett Cave on nearby Mount Anthony first. If she had taken her own life, it remained a mystery that no body was found, nor that she didn't return home to see her family.

An extensive search of the trail, nearby areas, and Everett Cave took place but there was no sign of Paula. Some locals bizarrely believed she had become a recluse living in secret on the mountain. There were even unsubstantiated rumours claiming she had eloped to nearby Canada, but she was never found.

Eerie disappearances

Three years later to the day on 1st December 1949, 68-year-old James Tedford took a bus back to Bennington after visiting family in the town of St. Albans, 150 miles away. He was a resident of the Bennington Soldiers Home and seen on the bus at the last stop before arriving at the town.

Between the last stop and Bennington, Tedford vanished under mysterious circumstances. His luggage and personal belongings were still on the rack in the bus, and a bus timetable was left open on his seat.

Multiple witnesses had seen him on the bus at the last stop before Bennington, even the bus driver, who didn't remember him leaving the vehicle at all. The mystery of James Tedford remains to this day with none of the circumstances of the disappearance making much sense.

If he had got off to use a toilet, no-one had seen him leave. If he got off believing the last stop before Bennington to be Bennington, then why did he leave all his belongings? And again, no-one saw him leave the bus and many witnesses claimed he was on the bus.

Then, to make things weirder, on 12th October 1950, eight-year-old Paul Jepson was playing in his family's pick-up truck when he too disappeared. When his parents returned from tending to local pigs at a yard where they worked, he was nowhere to be seen.

Hundreds of people formed large search parties to find Jepson but he was never found. A New Hampshire sheriff brought in bloodhounds to track the boy. Eerily, they tracked his scent to the very location where Paula had last been seen four years earlier.

Power of the mountain

Jepson's father spoke to the press of the lure of the mountains, and the power they had of being able to lure people to their deaths. He claimed that Jepson had talked of nothing else but the mountains for days before he disappeared.

Sixteen days later, on 28th October 1950, 53-year-old experienced hiker Frieda Langer disappeared in the same area. She was hiking with her cousin, Herbert Elsner, when after half hour, she slipped into a stream.

She asked Herbert to wait for her at the same spot, as she went back to the campsite to change her wet clothes.

When she didn't return, Herbert returned to camp and discovered that Frieda had never arrived. Once again, hundreds of searchers combed the area, including U.S. Army soldiers, helicopters and a light aircraft. No trace of her was found.

In May 1951, her decomposed body was discovered in the Somerset Reservoir, almost four miles from the camp, in an area that had previously been searched. Due to the condition of her remains, no cause of death could be concluded. It fuelled speculation as to what might have happened.

Curses and mysteries

The area in which the Bennington Triangle encapsulates, predates the colonisation of America. The history goes back to the Native Americans and their warnings of a great curse that lay over the land.

Native Americans refused to set foot on Glastenbury Mountain unless they were burying their dead. It was deemed an abnormal place due to 'four winds' that hit the top of the mountain in an eternal struggle for domination.

They also spoke of a sacred stone on the mountain's peak. If one was to stand on top of the stone to look out at the fantastic views of the landscape, then they would be swallowed by the mountain. The stone also swallowed those who dared to touch it.

There were also tales of giant hairy man – possibly early bigfoot sightings, and yes, you guessed it – aliens. The area is rich with UFO stories and paranormal activity, so much so that paranormal investigators consider the ghost town of Glastenbury to be a prime paranormal location.

In 1761, Benning Wentworth drew the boundaries of the town without ever seeing it, as the landscape was considered too harsh. He literally made it up, and the town never really took off because of it. In 1892, a sawmill worked named Henry McDowell got drunk and killed a co-worker.

He claimed there were voices coming from the mountain that told him to kill. He reached for a rock he believed was imbibed with special powers, and smashed his colleague over the head, killing him instantly. He was committed to an asylum but escaped and disappeared into thin air.

In 1894, one last ditch attempt was made to revive the ghost town and turn it into a tourist destination but work in the area resulted in extreme soil erosion which led to landslides. The resulting ground was virtually unusable, and again, developers abandoned the project.

In 1897, John Harbour went into a wooded area near Glastenbury to hunt. When his body was found, it was determined he had been shot dead by an unknown person. He had a loaded gun next to him and had been dragged several metres to the side of a stream. The murder remains unsolved.

In 2008, Bennington local Robert Singley took a familiar trail on the mountain before heading back.

Before he knew it, he found himself five miles away from the original trail. As the darkness set in, he tried to start a fire, but every branch he picked up was an animal bone.

He managed to survive the night, and when the morning broke through the clouds, he realised he had traversed the entire mountain without even knowing it. The trail he had taken was not familiar, and when he returned, he couldn't fathom how he reached the other side but deemed it to be a mysterious trail not on any map.

Bennington Monster

From the 18th Century to modern times, at least 40 people have died, been murdered, or mysteriously vanished in and around Glastenbury Mountain. The notion of multiple serial killers is unlikely, given that the age of the people who went missing in the 1945 to 1950 cluster are so varied.

Yet, without much evidence to show for the disappearances and discoveries, many theories and alternative explanations have been given down the years. Along with UFOs and curses, there are written reports of researchers believing the area is home to cross-dimensional wormholes.

Some consider the disappearances to be the work of the Bennington Monster, first sighted in the early 19th Century, and considered to be a cross between a bear and a man – bigfoot. In 1967, locals believed a wild-man lived in Everett Cave, where Paula was headed to when she vanished.

Other explanations include death and consumption by mountain cats, most likely a lynx or a bobcat, but they rarely attack humans. One report points to an animal called a catamount, which can be a puma or cougar, but they have been deemed extinct in the area since 1940.

Perhaps, the truth is less exotic, and has to do with the area's early history as a mining town. Many areas of the Glastenbury Mountain and ghost towns are full of unmarked mine shafts. Whoever goes off the trail could fall through one of the mineshafts to their death and never be found.

And then there's the weather. Many mountains across the world are known for their extreme changes in weather conditions. Glastenbury Mountain itself is known to change 40 degrees within a matter of hours. If one was to get caught out unprepared, it would be certain death, and their bodies consumed by wildlife.

There is a mystery at the heart of Bennington and the surrounding areas that continues to send imaginations sky high. The truth is that many people have vanished without a trace, leaving no evidence of their existence on earth. It's as if the mountain opened up and swallowed them whole.

The Wendigo Cannibal

A Cree Indian named Swift Runner became possessed by the spirit of the mythical Wendigo then killed and cannibalised his entire family, in the most famous case of Wendigo Psychosis.

The Wendigo myth

The Wendigo, sometimes referred to as Windigo, is a mythological creature or an evil spirit with a basis in Native Indian folklore. Historically, the Wendigo was thought to be roaming the East Coast forests of Canada, the Great Plains of North America, and the Great Lakes region of both.

In Native Indian mythology, the Wendigo is a malevolent spirit that can possess human beings, and usually takes the form of a creature with human characteristics. It's also believed to invoke a sensation of insatiable hunger, and the desire to cannibalise other humans.

Enter a Cree Indian named Swift Runner, who in 1878, in Fort Saskatchewan, Canada, became possessed by the Wendigo and proceeded to kill and eat his wife and five children. His eldest son had died of starvation just weeks before.

It became known as the most famous case of what is called Wendigo Psychosis, which is a psychological way of saying someone had been possessed by the Wendigo itself. Now a debated mental disorder, back in the late 19th Century, there was nothing but the Wendigo itself.

Swift Runner

Swift Runner was a Cree hunter and trapper who also served as a guide for the Northwest Mounted Police. He had received a good education and married the love of his life, who birthed six children. He was a big

Cree Indian, over six feet tall, and known to be a good family man who enjoyed whisky.

During the cold Winter of 1878 to 1879, a Wendigo visited Swift's family and ate them. After his eldest son had died of starvation, Swift became consumed with grief and hunger and systematically murdered his wife and five remaining children.

He cooked their bodies and ate their flesh, before leaving his Winter camp and heading back to Fort Saskatchewan in early 1879. When he returned without his wife and children, his relatives and friends became concerned, more so when Swift couldn't fully explain why they were not with him.

The Northwest Mounted Police were called in, along with Inspector Sévère Gagnon, who were given the grim task of investigating exactly what Swift had done. Gagnon and a small team of law enforcement officers trekked to Swift's Winter camp.

Swift calmly showed them the shallow grave of his eldest son and explained that he had died of starvation and he had no choice but to bury him. Gagnon ordered the grave to be opened where he found the bones of the boy.

As they searched the Winter camp, they became more concerned about the other human bones that were scattered all across the small settlement. Gagnon picked up an adult skull and showed Swift who told him without hesitation that it was the skull of his wife, and that the other bones were from his other family members.

Possession by the Wendigo

Swift had what he thought was a solid excuse for the murders, and it had started just weeks before the deaths. He first claimed he was haunted by sickening dreams of murder and death, and that the spirit of a Wendigo called on him to consume the people around him.

The Wendigo had crept into his mind and soul like a cancer, and before he knew it, had taken full control of his body. With the Wendigo in control, and no trace of Swift left, he proceeded to kill and eat his wife in front of the children.

He – or the Wendigo – manipulated the children into cooking and eating their mother, then ordered one of his sons to kill the youngest child, which he did. He then hung the small child by the neck and sliced off the flesh to be cooked.

Swift then resorted to killing off the rest of his children and consuming them the same way. It was down to Gagnon and the team to collect as much of the evidence as they could, including bones and flesh, and take them and Swift back to Fort Saskatchewan.

The trial began in the Summer of 1879 but was held at a Canadian court in the Fort. The judge and jury were made up of mostly white Canadians who did not believe in the myth of the Wendigo, even when presented with evidence of the creature by the Cree Indians.

The gallows

Swift didn't question the evidence against him and stated multiple times that he was guilty, and he had –

under the Wendigo's control – killed and eaten his family, because the Wendigo had an insatiable hunger that needed to be sated. He was sentenced to death.

At that time, Western Canada had not conducted a formal execution, and a police bugler – someone who played a bugle – was put in charge of the execution. He brought in some men to help build a gallows and recruited an elderly army pensioner to be the hangman.

On 20th December 1879, in the freezing, snowy darkness, a calm Swift was led to the gallows. Due to multiple delays, with the scaffolding not being ready, no straps to bind Swift's arms, and an accidental burning of the trap, Swift was forced to wait.

He sat with some of the jailers at a fire near the gallows and was recorded as saying; '*I could kill myself with a tomahawk and save the hangman further trouble.*' He thanked the police and his jailers for being so kind to him but shouted at the bugler and hangman for making him wait in the cold.

'I am no longer a man'

He didn't have to wait much longer as his execution was swiftly carried out in front of a 60-strong crowd. His last words were; '*I am no longer a man.*' The Cree Indians strongly believed in the Wendigo, as did many Native Americans at the time.

The Wendigo Psychosis element has been added to the story retrospectively, as it became a common term after Swift's execution. In the 20th Century, Wendigo

Psychosis was viewed by some researchers as a real disorder, that involved various levels of psychosis and mental issues.

There has long been disagreement as to whether Wendigo Psychosis was a fabrication or a real historical phenomenon. Interestingly, no case of Wendigo Psychosis has ever been studied, and most work on the issue has been done without direct contact with a sufferer.

The Wendigo is still well-known in the modern world, with many books, films, and TV series featuring versions of the myth. Swift Runner's case is the go-to example of so-called Wendigo psychosis. Though some believe he really had been possessed by the spirit of the creature.

The Liquid Matthew Clues

Shortly after a murder victim was found in the streets of Miami, detectives discovered a cryptic note inside a plastic bag, seemingly left by the killer, but the clues led them somewhere they didn't expect.

Follow the clues

Just north of Miami, in Hialeah, Florida, on 6th December 1983, two joggers on an evening run stumbled across the body of Colombian national Francisco Patino Gutierrez, in a small parking lot. Police cornered off the area and quickly removed Francisco's body due to an incoming rainstorm.

Throughout the night, Miami was hit with heavy rain, which police assumed would wipe away any evidence they were able to obtain from the scene. The next morning, once the rain had passed, investigators descended on the parking lot and got to work.

As the sun broke through the canopy, police technician Terry Anderson found a plastic bag tied to a nearby dumpster. Inside was a hand-written note that read;

'Once you're back on the track you'll travel in night. So prepare your old self for a terrible fright. Now the motive is clear and the victim is, too. You've got all the answers. Just follow the clues.'

Second clue

Investigators looked again at the crime scene photos, taken before the rainstorm, and discovered that the plastic bag had been there all along just away from the body. The clue itself was a mystery and made little sense but with nothing else to go on, they had to follow the clue.

Except the motive was not clear, as suggested in the note, and none of the answers to the police questions were obvious. Police Sergeant David Miller was handed the case and given the task of deciphering the clue.

Amazingly, Miller worked out what the clue meant within an hour and followed the cryptic directions he had been given. It led him to a speed limit sign on a nearby road, where he found another bag taped to the back of it, with another note inside. It read;

'Yes, Matthew is dead, but his body not felt. Those brains were not Matt's because his body did melt. For Billy threw Matt in some hot, boiling oil. To confuse the police for the mystery they did toil.'

Though the rhyming was good enough, the clue yet again made no sense, as the investigation already confirmed the deceased was named Francisco and not Matthew. Nor had Francisco's body shown any signs of coming into contact with hot oil, and his body certainly didn't melt.

Stumped by the cryptic nature of the second clue, Miller spent many days attempting to decipher it. He had followed the first clue easily enough but the second was seemingly unsolvable. There was only one thing for it; ask the public for help.

Liquid Matthew

Miller suspected the investigation had fallen into an elaborate game but still published the two notes in the Miami Herald and asked for people with information to contact him. In the middle of December, after days of false leads, Miller received two phone calls within an hour of each other.

Both calls were from members of a local church, near to where the body was found, and they had rather ordinary explanations for the notes. Both church members explained that four neighbourhood churches held a cooperative annual Halloween event every October.

Before the event, one of the members created a murder mystery game and wrote clues relating to various fictional crimes. These clues were put in plastic bags and hidden at various locations around the city.

Coincidentally, it had heavily rained the night of the event, and the notes were eventually forgotten about. They had been in the plastic bags to avoid them being damaged, which had kept them intact for the police to inadvertently find.

Despite the bizarreness of the clues, the church had nothing to do with the murders, and it was merely an unusual coincidence a man had been murdered near to one of the notes. It became known in the press as the 'Liquid Matthew' case, due to the note's mention of his body melting.

Miami drug wars

Police later discovered from an informant that Francisco was a seaman by trade and had travelled to Miami from Panama. He had brought 5kg of stolen cocaine with him. His murder was thought to be related to the cocaine theft but no suspect was ever found and the murder remains unsolved.

His death came at the peak of the Miami drug wars which were a series of armed conflicts from the late 1970s to the early 1980s. The battles between drug cartels, Police, DEA, and FBI, made Miami the most violent city in the United States at the time.

In 1980 alone, there were 573 murders, which increased to 621 in 1981. The drug wars resulted in over 1,200 murders, by way of shootings, stabbings, and bombings. It led to Miami briefly becoming the drug capital of the world and was considered a failed state by many people in power.

So it was with little respite, that the murder of Francisco would be remembered above hundreds of others, all because a church group were playing a murder mystery game for Halloween and forgot to collect the clues.

The Strange Case of Two Men Who Died Over Dinner

When two Frenchmen enjoying a Summer dinner were found dead at their garden table, police assumed murder was afoot in the small town of Authon-du-Perche, but the truth was far stranger.

Scene trapped in time

On 3rd August 2017, in the small town of Authon-du-Perche, 90 miles (150km) south-west of Paris, a mystery was developing that had gripped the local community. A day later, the story was making headlines around the world.

At the home of 69-year-old Lucien Pérot, both he and his friend, 38-year-old Olivier Boudin, had been enjoying a lavish dinner at an outside terrace table and had seemingly passed out from the evening before. Lucien was slumped in his chair, and Olivier was on the floor next to the table.

In the early hours of the morning, a passing neighbour noticed them but thought they were drunk and sleeping it off. When she returned a few hours later, she saw the two men in exactly the same positions.

Concerned, she moved closer and called out to them but there was no response. She called the police who arrived within minutes and found a scene trapped in time.

Lucien was slumped beside a half-finished dish of roast beef, beans, camembert, a half-eaten baguette, and a glass of wine. Olivier was lying on the ground, his half-eaten dinner resting on the table where he had been sitting.

Mysterious murder

The police were baffled as there were no obvious signs of attack but the fact that two men had died at the same time over dinner led them to believe a double murder had taken place. As they searched the rural property, they found no signs of robbery or forced entry.

Looking into their lifestyles, the pair had no enemies and nothing that made them targets for a murder or a pre-meditated hit. It turned out they lived relatively simple lives and were well-known and liked around the village.

Due to the position of the bodies, Lucien on the chair and Olivier on the ground, and with both meals half-eaten, it was deduced they had died at exactly the same time. But with no clear signs of attack, police were becoming more baffled, until they suggested the pair could have been poisoned.

The food was taking away to the famous Pasteur Research Institute in Paris where they underwent intense examination. While the testing was being carried out, a poisoning theory was doing the rounds in France and beyond.

On social media, people pointed to the beans as a possible way of poisoning someone as they would have been canned beforehand and the diners would not have noticed a small entry point where poison could have been injected into it.

But the Pasteur institute released their findings along with a hammer blow that threw out the poisoning theory. They concluded none of the food contained poison or was dangerous in any way. This meant that a mysterious murder was now on the table.

No explanation

The bodies were sent off to be autopsied in the hopes of discovering the truth of what had happened. The logical explanation was that the two men had been poisoned but with the food coming back negative, police had to consider other possibilities.

As the mystery exploded in the press and went viral online, the police struggled to find a motive and method of the murders. One neighbour mentioned a connection to the Mafia, which was explored but went nowhere, as the lives of the two men were easy to sift through.

Online theories suggested they were killed by an assassin of high skill who had killed them in such a manner that the method of murder would be impossible to uncover. This stretched from injections behind the ears, tiny explosive devices that stopped their hearts, electrical attack, psychic attack, and – yep, you guessed it – aliens.

The glaring truth was that two men had died at the same time, at the same table, and no-one could come up with a theory that worked and seemed logical. The only other hypothesis that gained traction was the two men had taken their own lives.

Yet, the same question was posed – how did they do it? Lucien and Olivier were said to be like father and son and had no obvious reason to take their own lives. Even if there were reasons to do so, the method was a mystery. Until the autopsy results came back.

Strange deaths

After days of wild theories, the investigation held a press conference to explain what had really happened. It turned out that the pair were not murdered, nor had they taken their own lives.

Lucien had literally bitten off more than he could chew and had swallowed a large piece of the delectable beef rib he had cooked for them. The autopsy found the piece of beef lodged in his throat and concluded that he had choked to death.

Triggered by the sight of his friend choking to death, Olivier suffered a major heart attack and fell off his chair to the ground where he died. He was known to have had a genetic heart condition which caused the attack at such a young age.

Armed with the truth, the locals were in some part grateful that the Mafia hadn't visited the tiny village, or that the deaths were not the result of murder. Though the scene looked like the perfect murder, and something out of an Agatha Christie novel, the truth turned out to be far more tragic – and stranger.

Before the autopsies were carried out, many people claimed with absolute conviction that the pair had been murdered, even pointing fingers at possible suspects. The strange death of Lucien and Olivier is perhaps a lesson that sometimes, not all is what it seems.

Bonus material

Bitesize Extras

Cosmic Karma

In 2011, in Immokalee, Florida, 33-year-old Nathaniel Coleman broke into a home and robbed the joint. He made off with thousands of dollars in jewellery and other pricey items.

Believing the robbery to be perfect, all he needed to do was cash in the items and make off with the money. But cosmic karma was about to intervene.

Nathaniel went to a nearby pawnbroker called Marilyn's Boutique and spread out his haul to see what price he could get. The store manager looked at the goods and immediately recognised them as her own.

Yep, Nathaniel had taken the stolen goods to a shop owned by the lady whose house he had broken into. Some criminals are stupid, others, like Nathaniel, have incredibly bad luck.

Burglar Trapped in Chimney

On 8th January 2022, in Montgomery County, Maryland, police responded to an unusual call from a man residing in a single-family home. He claimed that someone was trying to break into his house.

Police arrived but found nothing. An hour later, the man heard moaning inside the walls. Police returned and found a burglar stuck in the chimney of the property.

He had become wedged in the chimney above the fireplace after severely misjudging the width of it. Firefighters were called in to free him.

They had to dismantle the inner and outer wall brick by brick in order to reach the burglar. Photos were released to the press, including one with the man's legs hanging through a hole in the wall.

An hour later, the burglar was removed from the chimney and taken to hospital with a police escort. The unnamed man was later charged with attempted burglary and ordered to pay for the wall to be fixed.

There's only one man who's allowed to come down chimneys and we all know he doesn't do so on 8th January.

Death by Cow

In Caratinga, Brazil, in the Summer of 2013, while sleeping in bed with his wife, 45-year-old Joao Maria de Souza suffered an unfortunate fate when a cow fell through the ceiling of his home.

The cow had escaped from a local farm and climbed onto the corrugated tin roof, which was easily accessible as it backed onto a steep hill.

The roof collapsed and the one-ton animal dropped eight feet onto the sleeping de Souza. He was rushed to hospital with a broken leg but died from internal bleeding shortly after.

His wife, and the cow, survived, but it didn't stop the police investigating the 'crime' and subsequently charging the owner of the cow with involuntary manslaughter.

Being crushed by a cow in your own bed is the last way you expect to die.

Bizarre True Crime Volume 6 is also available as an eBook.

Out now!

Bibliography

A selected bibliography and resource.

BBC news. (2002) Art hoard worth $1.4bn destroyed. BBC News. http://news.bbc.co.uk/1/hi/entertainment/1990836.stm

BBC News. (2017) *Double death baffles French police*. https://www.bbc.co.uk/news/world-europe-40838168. BBC News.

BBC News. (2018) *Dennis Nilsen: Serial Killer Dies in Prison Aged 72* . BBC News. 13th May 2018.

Billock, Jennifer (2015). *Is a Jaws extra the victim in an unsolved murder case?* AV Club.

Biressi, Anita. Nunn, Heather. (2005) *Reality TV: realism and revelation*. Wallflower Press. ISBN: 9781904764045.

Carrasco, Matias. (2010) *They remember the 345 years of the death of the Quintrala*. Emol.com. https://www.emol.com/noticias/magazine/2010/01/16/3941 59/recuerdan-los-345-anos-de-la-muerte-de-la-quintrala.html

CBS Boston. (2017) *Triple Murderer Daniel LaPlante Must Wait 15 More Years Before Chance At Parole.* CBS Broadcasting Inc.

Citro, Joseph A. (1996) *Green Mountain Ghosts, Ghouls, and Unsolved Mysteries.* W.W. Norton & Co. ISBN: 9781881527503.

Citro, Joseph A. (1997) *Passing Strange: True Tales of New England Hauntings and Horrors*. Houghton Mifflin. ISBN: 9781576300596.

Courier Mail, The. (2011) *Convicted killer Luke Andrew Hunter worked for Queensland Health after escaping prison*. The Courier Mail. Queensland, Australia.

Day, Bek. (2021) *Cops' horrific discovery inside NSW home still haunts them*. https://www.news.com.au/lifestyle/real-life/true-stories/cops-horrific-discovery-inside-wa-home-still-haunts-them/news-story/73553ade114298cf8bfda4730d845e5b. News.com.au

Keane, Daniel. Martin, Patrick. (2019) *Life after death: Dark tourism and the future of Snowtown*. ABC News Australia.

Kiska, Tim. (1983) '*Robot firm liable in death*'. The Oregonian.

Lalor, Peter. (2002) *Blood Stain*. Allen & Unwin. ISBN: 1865088781.

Lewiston Daily Sun, The. (1983) 'Liquid Matthew' Case Is Solved. The Lewiston Daily Sun. https://news.google.com/newspapers?id=MnogAAAAIBAJ&sjid=p2cFAAAAIBAJ&pg=6003%2C3532486

Lisners, John. (1983) *House of Horrors: The Full Story of Dennis Andrew Nilsen*. Corgi Press. ISBN: 9780552124591.

Martin, Luis. (1989) *Daughters of the Conquistadores*. Southern Methodist University Press. ISBN: 9780870742972.

Masters, Brian. (2020) *Killing for Company: The Case of Dennis Nilsen*. Arrow. ISBN: 9781787466258.

McGarry, Andrew. (2019) *Did Orwell's nightmare Nineteen Eighty-Four inspire the Snowtown murders?* ABC News Australia.

New York Times, The. (1983) *Jury Awards $10 Million In Killing by Robot*. The New York Times.

Noce, Vincent. (2019) Serial art thief Stéphane Breitwieser arrested—again. https://www.theartnewspaper.com/2019/02/14/serial-art-thief-stephane-breitwieser-arrestedagain. The Art Newspaper

Oxer, Charles Ralph. (1975) *Women in Iberian Expansion Overseas 1415-1815*. Oxford University Press. ISBN: 9780195198171.

Salonga, Robert. (2018) *Suspect in 1974 Stanford church slaying kills self with detectives closing in.* The Mercury News. https://www.mercurynews.com/2018/06/28/sheriff-suspect-in-infamous-1974-stanford-chapel-murder-shoots-self-as-detectives-close-in/

Saslow, Rachel (2011). *CT scans help reconstruct faces of unidentified victims to solve cold cases.* Washington Post.

Smallman, Shawn. (2014) *Dangerous Spirits: The Windigo in Myth and History.* Heritage House Publishing Company. ISBN: 9781772030334.

Smith, Rupert. (2002) *The price of fame.* The Guardian Newspaper. https://www.theguardian.com/media/2002/nov/18/tvandradio.television.

Stickley, Tony. (2011) *Murderer next door.* Cairns Post.

Teicher, Morton I. (1961) *Windigo Psychosis: A Study of Relationship between Belief and Behaviour among the Indians of North-eastern Canada.* The 1960 Annual Spring Meeting of the American Ethnological Society. University of Washington Press.

Terry, Maury. (1987) *The Ultimate Evil: An Investigation into America's Most Dangerous Satanic Cult.* Doubleday. ISBN: 038523452X.

Terry, Maury. (1989) *The Ultimate Evil-The Truth about the Cult Murders Son of Sam and Beyond.* Bantam Books. ISBN: 0553276018.

Tweedie, Neil. (2006) *Nilsen Describes How he Murdered his First Victim.* The Daily Telegraph. London.

Wakatama, Giselle. (2020) *Remembering Katherine Mary Knight, Australia's 'female Hannibal Lecter', 20 years on.* ABC Newcastle.

Wehrstein, KM. (2017) *'Pollock Twins (reincarnation case)'.* Psi Encyclopedia. The Society for Psychical Research. https://psi-encyclopedia.spr.ac.uk/articles/pollock-twins-reincarnation-case.

Willsher, Kim. (2017) *Post-mortems solve strange case of French pair who died at dinner.*
https://www.theguardian.com/world/2017/aug/09/mysterious-case-two-men-found-dead-authon-du-perche-french-village-solved. The Guardian.

Photo and image credits:

Enrique Meseguer, Jeff Orth, CDD20, Nika Akin, Coquito Clemente, Marko Lovric, Alexas Fotos, Hermann Traub, Leo (Leo 2014), Sam Williams, Péter Kadlec, Gerd Altmann, Engin Akyurt, Brigitte (Art Tower), Etienne Marais, Prettysleepy Art. Designs by Twelvetrees Camden. Images are used as a representation of the story content and do not relate specifically to the crime.

Full passage from Ecclesiastes 12, one through eight, from the Chuck Morgan story.

1. Remember now thy Creator in the days of thy youth, while the evil days come not, nor the years draw nigh, when thou shalt say, I have no pleasure in them;

2. While the sun, or the light, or the moon, or the stars, be not darkened, nor the clouds return after the rain:

3. In the day when the keepers of the house shall tremble, and the strong men shall bow themselves, and the grinders cease because they are few, and those that look out of the windows be darkened,

4. And the doors shall be shut in the streets, when the sound of the grinding is low, and he shall rise up at the voice of the bird, and all the daughters of music shall be brought low;

5. Also when they shall be afraid of that which is high, and fears shall be in the way, and the almond tree shall flourish, and the grasshopper shall be a burden, and desire shall fail: because man go-eth to his long home, and the mourners go about the streets:

6. Or ever the silver cord be loosed, or the golden bowl be broken, or the pitcher be broken at the fountain, or the wheel broken at the cistern.

7. Then shall the dust return to the earth as it was: and the spirit shall return unto God who gave it.

8. Vanity of vanities, saith the preacher; all is vanity.

Full victim list related to the Bodies in the Barrels story.

Clinton Trezise, 22, killed 31st August 1992, body found 16th August 1994.

Ray Davies, 26, killed December 1995, body found 26th May 1999.

Suzanne Allen, 47, died November 1996, body found 23rd May 1999.

Michelle Gardiner (Born Michael Gardiner), 19, killed September 1997, body found 20th May 1999.

Vanessa Lane (Born Barry Lane), 42, killed October 1997, body found 20th May 1999.

Thomas Trevilyan, 18, killed 5th November 1997, body found 5th November 1997 in Kersbrook.

Gavin Porter, 29, killed April 1998, body found 20th May 1999.

Troy Youde, 21, killed August 1998, body found 20th May 1999.

Frederick Brooks, 18, killed September 1998, body found 20th May 1999.

Gary O'Dwyer, 29, killed October 1998, body found 20th May 1999.

Elizabeth Haydon, 37, killed 21st November 1998, body found 20th May 1999.

David Johnson, 24, killed 9th May 1999, body found 20th May 1999.

Look for more in the Bizarre True Crime Series from Ben Oakley & Twelvetrees Camden

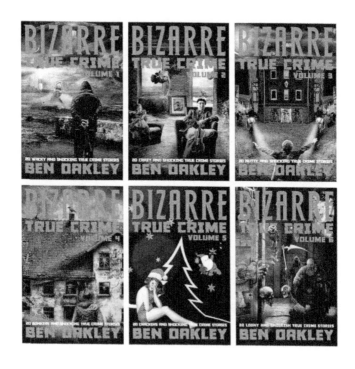

OUT NOW!

Printed in Great Britain
by Amazon

75959554R00108